50 SIMPLE THINGS KIDS CAN DO TO SAVE THE EARTH

The Ear̶̶̶̶̶̶̶̶̶̶p

Illustration̶̶̶ Montez
and by L̶ ̶̶̶e Bodger

Andrews McMeel
Publishing, LLC
Kansas City • Sydney • London

This is for all kids, but especially Jesse, Sophie,
Gideon, Sam, Joshua, Magdalena, and Avery

Andrews McMeel Publishing, LLC
an Andrews McMeel Universal company
1130 Walnut Street, Kansas City, Missouri 64106

10 11 12 13 RR2 10 9 8 7 6 5 4 3 2

Library of Congress Cataloging-in-Publication Data

The new 50 simple things kids can do to save the earth / the Earthworks
Group ; illustrations by Michele Montez and Lorraine Bodger.
    p. cm.
ISBN: 978-0-7407-7746-2
 1. Environmental protection--Citizen participation--Juvenile literature.
I. Montez, Michele, ill. II. Bodger, Lorraine, ill. III. Earth Works Group
(U.S.) IV. Title: new fifty simple things kids can do to save the earth.
TD171.7.N48 2008
363.7'0525--dc22

2009001277

www.andrewsmcmeel.com

Created and packaged by the EarthWorks Group
Illustrated by Michele Montez
and by Lorraine Bodger

We've provided a great deal of information about practices and products
in our book. In most cases we've relied on advice, recommendations, and
research by others whose judgments we consider accurate and free from
bias. However, we can't and don't guarantee the results. This book offers
you a start. The responsibility for using it ultimately rests with you.

ACKNOWLEDGMENTS

Special thanks to Sharon, Sophie, and Jesse Javna for helping write this book. John Javna and the EarthWorks Group would also like to thank:

- Linda Glaser
- Michele Montez
- Judy Plapinger
- Phil Catalfo
- Chris Calwell
- Andy Sohn
- Marydele Donnelly
- Jeff Altemus
- Fritz Springmeyer

- Lorraine Bodger
- Claudia Bauer
- Jinnee Joos
- Christine DeGueron
- Dorothy O'Brien
- Karina Lutz
- Lisa Epstein, and the entire 1990 5th grade class at John Muir Elementary School in Berkeley, California

and a host of others who made the book successful in the 1990s.

CONTENTS

A NOTE TO KIDS

There are lots of things that grown-ups are allowed to do, but most kids aren't: Stay up past 11:30... wear short sleeves when it's raining...eat chocolate for dinner. The list goes on. But here's one important thing grown-ups and kids can *both* do: Take care of our planet.

Is that a surprise? You may think protecting the environment is too big a job for kids to handle, but that's just not true. If you want to cut back on pollution, or help save an animal from extinction, or help protect a forest, there's absolutely *nothing* stopping you! There are lots of fun ways to seriously improve our planet just by replacing a few things around your house, or by changing a habit or two.

For kids who want to know exactly what you *can* do, this is the perfect book! It's got lots of great ideas and projects to try at home, at your school, or around your neighborhood. It even has cool things to show your friends. And don't be shy about sharing it with your teacher. You'd be surprised at how interested grown-ups are in what kids have to say, especially when it comes to saving our Earth.

So, raise your voice and have a say in what's happening to the planet! You have the power to make a difference, and hopefully have a blast doing it. Thanks for showing you care, and don't forget: We're all rooting for you, 'cause it's *our* planet too!

Your friend,
    Sophie Javna (age 15)

P.S. The computer is your friend! There are lots of awesome links in the book that will help you along the way, so be sure to check some of them out.

TO PARENTS AND TEACHERS

When we sat down to write *50 Simple Things Kids Can Do to Save the Earth* 20 years ago, there weren't many children's environmental books in print. The ones that did exist tended to talk down to their audience...or to tell kids what they'd be able to do *later on*, when they were older.

That didn't make sense to us. As we wrote in our introduction at the time, "In our experience, kids are not only willing, but very eager to do their part. But they need information, encouragement, and the sense that they have the power to make a difference."

The challenge, we decided, was to create a new kind of environmental how-to book—one that would give kids real things to do and explain the real results....a book that could make it clear to young readers that their actions have a lasting effect on the world *right now*. So the litmus tests for including a "Simple Thing" in the book became: "Is it something kids can do on their own?" and "Does the action have an immediate impact they can understand?"

Apparently, we did something right. There have been hundreds of similar books published since 1990 (some have even tried to appropriate the "50 Simple" title), but ours is the best-selling kids' environmental book of all time. And to our amazement, it has continued to sell, despite the fact that until now, it has never been updated. To keep it relevant, and to make sure it still provides good information, we've created this new edition.

THE UPDATED 50 SIMPLE THINGS

It may not be especially good news, but it turns out that most of the issues we included 20 years ago are still valid. So we haven't had to change the book drastically. We've updated stats, of course, and replaced about 20% of the "Simple Things" with new ones. We've also included a little info about "school activism" whenever possible, and added a feature called *Amaze Your Friends*. But the biggest change in the book is the addition of web sites. The Internet barely existed when we first published this book; today, it is a primary educational tool.

So, whereas in 1990 we offered addresses and phone numbers to readers who wanted more info, today we offer URLs (web addresses)...and there are hundreds of URLs in this book; we've included the best kids' web sites we could find for each subject. Unfortunately, URLs are sometimes quite long and may be challenging for younger children. So we hope you'll help them access the web sites. It's also inevitable that at least a few of the sites will eventually go offline. We apologize in advance, but there's no way we can control that.

Generally, it isn't necessary to type in "www" anymore, so we haven't included it on our URL listings—unless we know it's essential (you *do* need it on some government sites). However, if your kids can't access a site, we suggest that you try it with either the "www," or "http://" only. If that still doesn't work, check to see if your computer is automatically inserting one of these prefixes. Some sites actually won't work with a "www," but your computer doesn't know that, and might add "www" to the URL. But don't worry: If a site goes down, or there's a trick to access it, we'll post it prominently on our web site, *50simplekids.com*.

Speaking of our web site: We encourage you to use *50simplekids.com*. You'll find lots of great new entries for kids (constantly updated!)...plus a special resource section for teachers and parents, along with blogs where you can discuss environmental education with other adults.

Twenty years later, it's more important than ever to give our children the tools and motivation they need to take care of our planet. We hope this new edition of *50 Simple Things* will assist you in that crucial task.

WHAT'S

HAPPENING

CLIMATE CHANGE

HOT BLANKET

The Earth is surrounded by a blanket of gases that acts like a greenhouse—it lets the sun's heat in, then traps it close to the Earth. That's good—we can't live without warmth.

WHAT'S GOING ON

Factories, electric power plants, and cars are putting too much of one of these gases—carbon dioxide (CO_2)—into the air.

MANY CHANGES

Scientists believe this extra layer of CO_2 is changing the planet's climate, because the "blanket" is holding in too much heat. People call this the *greenhouse effect*, or *global warming*.

WHAT CAN HAPPEN

If the Earth's temperature gets hotter by just a few degrees, polar ice can melt, raising the level of the ocean and wiping out islands and coastal areas.

THAT'S NOT ALL

Other things can happen, too. For example, when the ocean warms up, sea life can die…there can be more hurricanes…places that grow most of our food can get too warm to grow crops.

THE LATEST REPORT

Polar ice *is* melting today… and much faster than scientists expected. What will happen next? No one knows, but we have to do *something*!

Every kid can help stop global warming by using less energy, protecting and planting trees, and recycling. This book is full of tips on how to do it.

WATER POLLUTION

WATER, WATER

The planet Earth is mostly water. Oceans cover the biggest part of it—and there are lakes, rivers, streams, and even water underground. All life on Earth—from the littlest bug to the biggest whale—depends on this water. It's precious.

But we're not doing a very good job of keeping water clean. In many places, the water has become polluted.

RIVERS AND LAKES

Rivers and lakes are polluted by garbage, or by poisonous chemicals that are dumped right into them.

UNDERGROUND

Underground water can be polluted by gasoline or other harmful liquids that seep into the ground. Some fertilizers and pesticides used on farms or lawns leak down through the dirt, too.

THE SEAS

The ocean, which is a home to so much life, has been used as a place to dump garbage and poisonous chemicals for a long time. It's getting polluted, too.

OUR MISSION

We need to save our water, to keep it clean and healthy so people, plants, and animals will always have some to drink. And so fish and other creatures will have a place to live.

To learn more about what you can do to save water—and keep it clean and healthy—turn to *Preserving Our Oceans, Rivers, Lakes, and Streams.*

WASTING ENERGY

IMPORTANT STUFF!

Practically everything we do uses energy. We need it for lights, stoves, refrigerators, hot water, heating, air-conditioning, cars, trucks, planes, and lots more.

IT WON'T LAST

Where do we get our energy? Mostly from oil, natural gas, and coal. These things are dug out of the Earth. There is a limited amount of each...so in the future, we will run out of them. That's one reason we need to be careful how we use energy.

POLLUTION HAPPENS

Another reason to be careful about wasting energy is that when we burn gas, oil, and coal (and some other sources of energy), we create the pollution that causes global warming and smog. So, using less energy means a cleaner environment.

SAVING ENERGY

The easiest way to use less energy is to *conserve* it. That means not using energy we don't need. Another good way: we can use efficient products that are especially designed to use less energy.

EXTRA ENERGY

There are many ways to conserve energy. Every time you turn off a light, or walk instead of drive, or turn down the heat, you save energy and reduce pollution.

OTHER CHOICES

Another way to be energy-smart is to support people who are working to create clean energy from the sun, wind, and water. This energy doesn't pollute or use up our treasures the way oil, coal, and gas do.

Can you save energy? Yes! Go to *Using Energy Wisely* and *Guarding Our Buried Treasures* to get started.

AIR POLLUTION

THE OLD DAYS

Until about 150 years ago, the air was pure and clean—perfect for the people and animals of the Earth to breathe.

FACTORIES

Then people started building factories. Those factories and many of the things they make, like cars, put a lot of harmful gases into the air. Then people started driving cars, which added more pollution to the air.

TODAY

Today the air is so polluted in some places that it's not always safe to breathe!

THE BROWN STUFF

Many cities around the world have air filled with a pollution called "smog." This is so strong in some places that the air, which should be a beautiful blue, actually looks brown.

DOWN WITH POLLUTION!

Polluted air is is not only bad for people and animals, but for trees and other plants as well. And in some places it's even damaging farmers' crops—the food we eat. So it's important for us to "clean up our act," and clean up the air we breathe.

Everyone can help keep our air clean and safe. It's even fun! You can plant a tree, ride your bike, and even send an e-mail about clean air to a newspaper editor. For more ideas on how to clean up our air, keep reading!

DISAPPEARING ANIMALS

THE PEOPLE BOOM

Every day, there are more and more people living on Earth. All these people need room to live. So, they move into places that are already homes for plants and animals. Forests are cut down, and wild areas are filled with houses and stores.

WHAT HAPPENS

When people move into new land, the plants and animals that live there can become endangered—which means that because there's no place for them to live, they begin to disappear. Some even become extinct—which means that they all die out, and are gone from the Earth forever.

WHAT CAN HAPPEN

We enjoy pictures and stories about the dinosaurs who lived on the earth many millions of years ago.

They're all extinct now. That could happen to elephants, zebras, redwood trees, frogs, butterflies, robins, or goldfish…or other animals, if we're not careful.

OUR MISSION

Let's keep the Earth green and healthy and full of millions of wonderful creatures!

Can you help animals? Yes! To find out how, check out *Preserving Our Oceans, Rivers, Lakes, and Streams, Protecting Animals,* and *Keeping the Earth Green.*

LOSING FORESTS, FOOD, AND FARMS

GREEN IS GOOD
We depend on healthy plants for essential things, from food…to air. That's right—the life-giving oxygen we breathe in is what plants breathe out! In fact, a mature tree can supply enough oxygen in a year for two people!

PLANTS CURE
Plants also give us important medicine. Some of the drugs that fight diseases like cancer come from plants in tropical rainforests.

LET'S EAT!
And of course, without the plants farmers give us, what would we eat? Corn, carrots, cauliflower, lettuce, tomatoes, wheat, and practically everything else in your kitchen come from farms.

LESS AND LESS
The whole world needs more forests and farms. But overall, we're losing them instead. Every minute, for example, the world loses 100 acres of rainforest!

BYE-BYE FARMS
In the U.S. we lose 2 acres of mostly prime farmland every minute of the day! We build houses and factories on the land instead. That means we have fewer places to grow our food!

BYE-BYE TOPSOIL
The rich soil we need to make things grow is called *topsoil*…and we're losing *that*, too. When too many trees are cut down in one place, for example, topsoil can wash away

Can you help keep the Earth green and healthy? You bet—and your friends and family can, too! See *Make New Dirt* and *Keeping the Earth Green*.

RUNNING OUT
OF WATER

MOST IMPORTANT

Nobody can live without water. You need it to drink, to wash, to cook, and so on.

LESS TO USE

There are more and more people on Earth every day. But there isn't more water —we have the same amount today that we did 1,000 years ago! So that means there's less for each person to use.

WATER HOGS

The average American uses as much as 175 gallons of water every day. In other countries people use less.

IT'S A WASTE

A lot of what we use is water we don't really need. For example, we often let water run when we don't need to. Or we use too much water on our lawns…or we have toilets and showers that use more than they should.

HARD FACTS

In many parts of the world, people don't have enough clean water to drink. Unfortunately, that problem will keep getting worse. With global warming growing, there will be less and less fresh water every year.

WATER-SAVERS

We owe it to others in the world to be careful about how much water we use. The more we save, the more there is to go around.

EXTRA BENEFITS

Saving water saves energy and cuts pollution, too. To make the water drinkable, we have to treat it with chemicals. And to get it to our houses, we have to use energy to pump it.

It's easy to save water. Check out *Preserving Our Oceans, Rivers, Lakes, and Streams*.

TOO MUCH STUFF

WE'VE GOT A LOT!

Take a look around your home. See all the stuff your family has? You're a part of a very special group: We own more things than any people in the world.

THROWAWAYS?

We also throw more things away than anyone else. In other parts of the world where they have less, they expect to keep things and reuse them. But in the U.S. it's normal to use some things just once, then toss them out. We call these things "disposable." This makes lots of extra garbage, and uses up a lot of the Earth's treasures.

NOT ENOUGH STUFF

What would happen if everyone tried to live this way? Well, there are about 6 billion people on the planet. But there's only enough for about 2 billion of them to live the way we do. That means around 2/3 of the world's population would have nothing at all!

GOOD NEWS

We can follow the 3 R's—Reduce, Reuse, and Recycle. That means we can Reduce the amount of stuff we use or buy…Reuse what we've got instead of throwing it away…and then make sure valuable materials get used again by Recycling them.

EARTH SAVERS

When you use less stuff, you save the Earth in many ways—you use less energy, waste less of the Earth's treasures, create less pollution, save water, and more!

You and everyone you know can learn to use less stuff. To find out more, see *Guarding Our Buried Treasures* and *Be a Paper Saver.*

WHAT KIDS SAY

ABOUT WATER POLLUTION

"If we the people pollute the water, we will kill the fish and the animals that live nearby will die, too. Then it will make the food chain out of order. Then we will die because the food chain is not in order."

—*Joey Leichter, age 10*

"If people want to live and be healthy, they need to care a hoot about our lakes."

—*Emika Porter, age 10*

ABOUT AIR POLLUTION

"People shouldn't use cars as much, so that it doesn't pollute the air. If we're not careful, no one will be able to breathe the air and everyone will have to wear gas masks."

—*Regan Horner, age 10*

"No gases! No air pollution! It's life or death."

—*Jess Hornstein, age 10*

"Air pollution is devastating. It is the worst thing. I hate the way it makes the air smell."

—*Emika Porter, age 10*

ABOUT WASTING ENERGY

"Energy is so important. If we didn't have it, we couldn't stay warm in the winter, or cool in the summer. We wouldn't have lights, or TVs, or practically anything that makes our lives easy and fun. So what I don't understand, is why do we waste it so much?"

—*Billy Shutema, age 10*

ABOUT WILDLIFE

"Trees are getting cut down....But we need the trees. And wild animals need the trees too, to live in."

—*Shannon Lemmons, age 10*

"We need to help animals so they will not become extinct."

—*Shiquela Smith, age 10*

ABOUT RECYCLING

"We have to stop buying things that we can only use once and then throw away."

—*Karen Leason, age 10*

"There is too much garbage in the world. The landfills will get so overcrowded that we will be living around garbage every day....If we would recycle more, we wouldn't have such a BAD garbage problem!"

—*Lauren Weber, age 10*

ABOUT GLOBAL WARMING

"I think global warming and the greenhouse effect are very bad! What do we want the earth to become, a flaming ball?"

—*Adam Adler, age 11*

"Why are we letting the greenhouse effect happen? It doesn't make sense. I think it's time we got together and kept our home the right temperature for living things."

—*Jessamine Catalfo, age 10*

GUARDING OUR
OUR

BURIED
TREASURES

TREASURE
THOUGHTS

Buried treasure! It makes you think of pirates and hidden chests full of gold.

But gold is only one of the many buried treasures in our Earth. There are many wonderful things that this planet has been storing up for billions of years. How many can you name? There's oil, iron, silver, sand, aluminum, copper…you could go on and on.

These treasures are a gift to us. We heat our homes with them in the winter, we make them into tools, we cook with them…in fact there's practically nothing we don't use them for.

But there's a limited amount of them. When we use them all up, there will be no more. So it's up to us to decide—what should we do with them? Should we take them all out of the Earth and turn them in to things we don't really need? Or should we save them, so we—and all the creatures of the Earth—will still have them?

Sounds like a silly question…yet, we haven't asked it often enough.

Now it's your turn to ask the question—and come up with the answers. After all, the Earth's buried treasures belong to you, too.

1. RECYCLE GLASS

Take a Guess:
What is glass made of?
A) Frozen water B) Sand C) Yogurt

Lightbulbs, windows, TVs, mirrors…What do they all have in common? Glass.

Look around. See how much glass we use.

Now here's an amazing fact: We throw most of our glass away.

Every month, we toss out enough glass bottles and jars to fill up a *giant skyscraper*!

You probably think this doesn't make much sense, since we're just making more garbage…and wasting the Earth's treasures besides.

And you're right.

This is especially true because we can reuse all those bottles and jars—we can recycle them!

Did You Know

• It's pretty simple to make glass. You mix sand and a few other natural materials (*feldspar, ash*, and *limestone*), put them in a really hot furnace, and melt them. Presto! You've got glass.

• But there's another way to do it: You can just melt down old bottles and jars. This is better for the Earth because old glass melts at a lower temperature than the materials in new glass. So melting old glass for recycling takes a lot less energy, and creates less pollution, than making new glass from scratch.

Answer: B. That's right, glass is made from heating and melting sand.

- In fact, the energy you save by recycling *just one bottle* could light a 100-watt lightbulb for four hours! And it makes 80% less waste than new glass.

- For thousands of years, glass was considered precious. Then we got so good at making it that we started thinking of it as garbage. Now we throw out billions of bottles and jars every year! Think of how much energy and pollution we could save by recycling!

What You Can Do

- It's easy to recycle. When you finish with a bottle or jar, lightly rinse it out with water to get rid of leftover food or drink, which attracts ants and other pests.
- Take off caps, corks, or lids—they can't be recycled with glass. But it's okay to leave paper or plastic labels on—they burn or blow off when the glass is recycled.
- "Neck rings"—the part of the bottle caps that are still on the bottle necks—can be left on, too.
- Don't forget to pick up bottles when you find them and take them home to recycle. But wash off the sand and dirt.
- Check out Simple Thing #7, *Be a Recycling Detective*, to find out where to recycle in your area. Then make a plan with your family to recycle your bottles and jars.

- Important: You can't recycle *windows, drinking glasses, vases, mirrors,* or *lightbulbs.* They're made of different kinds of glass that can't be melted down with bottles and jars.

Amaze Your Friends

- Show them the coolest way to recycle glass: the Glass Bottle House on Prince Edward Island, Canada. It's just what it sounds like—a house made of bottles! See: *maisonsdebouteilles.com/gallery.cfm*

- If that's not amazing enough, check out the Wat Pa Maha temple in Thailand. It's made of over one million bottles! *inhabitat.com/2008/10/27/temple-of-a-million-bottles/*

See for Yourself

- **Ollie Recycles.** This is a British site. Some of their stats are different from ours, but a lot are the same: *ollierecycles.com/uk/html/glass.html*

- **A great kids' video** about recycling glass: *recyclenow.com/fun_stuff/index.html*

- **Just for kids.** A very simple version of how glass gets recycled: *ecy.wa.gov/programs/swfa/kidspage/glass.html*

- **Is that all glass?** Yes, and it's being recycled! *getunderground.com/global_images/albums/GLASS1.jpg*

*There's a lot more to see and do at **50simplekids.com***

2. TOO MANY WATER BOTTLES

Take a Guess:
What's the difference between most bottled water and tap water?
A) Tap water is red   B) Tap water can tap dance   C) Nothing

When you're really thirsty, cold water is great. Ah-h-h—there's nothing like it!

But hold on…If you're drinking water from a plastic bottle, it might not be good for you…and it definitely isn't good for the Earth. Really!

Did you know that chemicals used in some plastic water bottles aren't safe, especially for kids?

On top of that, we use up millions of gallons of oil and create plenty of pollution just making bottles for bottled water. Then we use more energy trucking them to stores. Finally, we just throw most of these bottles away.

And what does using up the Earth's treasures this way get us? Water that's about the same as the water we already get right out of our own faucets! Crazy, huh?

Did You Know

• Believe it or not, 40% of bottled water comes from exactly the same source as tap water. But the government tests

C. In most cases, there's little or no difference at all.

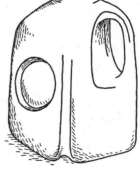

your tap water much more often, and much more strictly, than it tests bottled water. So, tap water is probably safer to drink!

- Until about 50 years ago, hardly anyone used plastic bottles for drinks. Today, Americans throw away more than 2-1/2 million plastic water bottles *every hour*...even though they're easy to recycle.

- You can tell a water bottle is recyclable by the #1 in a recycling symbol on the bottle. This means it's made of a plastic called *PET*. (Soda bottles are also #1.)

What You Can Do

At Home

- Be the first one in your school or neighborhood to *Take Back the Tap* by drinking good old tap water instead of bottled water.

- Instead of one-use plastic bottles, carry a reusable water bottle made of stainless steel or #5 polypropylene plastic.

- If you don't like the way your tap water tastes, get your folks to try using a water filter. It makes a big difference!

- And any time you use *any* plastic bottles, try to recycle them. See Simple Thing #7 for more info on how to find out which plastics can be recycled in your area.

• Recycling note: If a plastic bottle (like a milk jug) has a #2 inside a recycling symbol, it's a plastic called *high-density polyethylene* (HDPE) and is probably recyclable in your area.

At School

• Start a *Plastic Bottle Recycling Program*, like the students at Greystone Elementary School in Birmingham, Alabama. They created a "pilot" recycling program that collected 9,200 plastic water bottles in two months. It was so successful that other schools in the area started doing it, too!

Amaze Your Friends

Go online; show them what can be made from recycled plastic bottles, like clothes (*eartheasy.com/wear_ecospun.htm*) and carpet (*npr.org/templates/story/story.php?storyId=10874230*).

See for Yourself

• **Sign the Break the Bottled Water Habit pledge** (ask your family and friends to sign it, too): *water.newdream.org*

• **Unrecycled bottles!** *youtube.com/watch?v=OZbTXDkrD1o*

• **Bottled vs. tap water:** *newdream.org/marketplace/water.php*

• **Recycle at school:** *p2pays.org/recycleguys/guidelines.asp* or *dosomething.org/actnow/actionguide/start-a-school-recycling-program*

3. DON'T CAN IT!

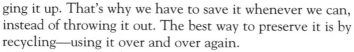

Take a Guess:
How many times can one aluminum can be recycled?
A) Never   B) Just once   C) Again and again and again

Before a soda can gets to the store...before it has soda in it...before it's even a can... it is part of the Earth!

Soda cans are made of a metal called aluminum. It is very important to us.

We need aluminum for airplanes, cars, bicycles, and many household items—not just for soda.

There's still aluminum in the ground, but it won't be a buried treasure forever if we keep digging it up. That's why we have to save it whenever we can, instead of throwing it out. The best way to preserve it is by recycling—using it over and over again.

Did You Know

• Americans use over 100 billion soda cans every year and recycle more than half of them. That's good...but we can do better—we could recycle all of them!

• Here's how aluminum is recycled: Soda cans and other aluminum products like cat food cans and aluminum foil are collected and sent to factories, where they're ground into little metal chips. Then they're melted down and turned into solid aluminum bars.

• The bars are rolled into sheets of aluminum, which are then sold to can makers...who make new cans out of them.

Answer: C. Aluminum cans can be recycled over and over and over and over and over...

• They filled 18 big garbage bags with cans and sold them to a local recycler for $1 a pound. Then they gave the money to a village in Africa that had no drinking water, to help people there drill a well. So...Is there someone you would like to help? Start recycling cans!

Amaze Your Friends

See how many cans Americans throw away every year.

• Take your friends to a supermarket and find the aisle with the soda and beer cans in it. Count out 58 six-packs. That's quite a lot. In fact, it's 348 cans; there may not even be that many in the store. But if there are, it will take you a while to count them all.

• When you're done, take a look at all the cans you've counted. That's how many the average person in this country uses every year!

• Imagine throwing half the cans out. What a waste. Now imagine using them again. Much better!

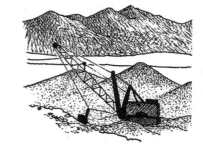

See for Yourself

• **Recycling in England:** *thinkcans.net*

• **Click on "Garbage & Recycling":** *pbskids.org/ eekoworld*

• **Meet Al the Can:** *recycle.novelis.com/Recycle/EN/Kids*

• **See what mining aluminum does to the Earth:** *www. container-recycling.org/alumfact/dirty.htm*

• **Your teachers** can learn can recycling at school at: *consrv.ca.gov/dor/rre/kids/Documents/RecycleProgram.pdf*

There's a lot more to see and do at **50simplekids.com**

4. PRECYCLE IT!

Take a Guess:

Over half the plastic we buy and throw away each year is just packaging. What happens to it when it's thrown away?

A) Nothing—it just sits there and clutters up the Earth
B) It gets up and starts dancing   C) It watches TV

Did you ever stop to think that when you buy something packaged in plastic or cardboard, you're actually buying and paying for the thing, *plus* garbage?

It sounds ridiculous, doesn't it? But that's what happens. You tear off the packaging and stuff it right in the garbage!

If it's plastic packaging, it's made from one of the Earth's greatest buried treasures—oil. It's been underground for millions of years...and it may even have been part of a dinosaur once! Think about that.

If we turn oil into plastic, we can never change it back; it can never be part of the Earth again.

So whenever you buy a toy, some food, or anything...you have a terrific chance to help the Earth! Look around. See how things are packaged. Make careful choices. You can do it!

Answer: A. Plastic will be around for thousands of years, at least. What a mess!

Did You Know

• Each American throws away about 60 pounds of plastic packaging every year! Think about how much you weigh. Now think about how much 60 pounds is. That's a lot of plastic.

• About 1/3 of all the garbage we throw away is packaging.

• Practically all the plastic ever made on Earth is still here. That's right! The plastic packages your mom bought way back when she was a girl are still on the Earth, buried in a garbage dump somewhere...or floating in the ocean!

What You Can Do

• Use the *precycling* test: *Before* you decide what to buy, think about how much packaging you'll have to throw away.

• Look for packages that can be reused or recycled (instead of thrown in the garbage).

• Even better: Buy packages made of materials that have *already* been recycled. For example, cardboard egg cartons are almost always made of recycled paper...and you can reuse them: Egg cartons make great containers for planting seeds.

• Talk to your family about buying food in *bulk*—which means buying a lot of it at once. When you buy one large bottle of apple juice, for example, you'll get as much juice as two or more small bottles, but you'll use less packaging.

Amaze Your Friends

• If they're like most people, they don't really know how much packaging they use. So, challenge them to keep a big box or bag handy at home for one week. Use it to collect all the packaging their families throw away. Then see what's there. They'll probably be shocked to find out. Try it yourself, too!

See for Yourself

• **The PlanetPals site** includes their "Top Ten Ways Kids Can Precycle": *planetpals.com/precycle.html*

• **Old-time general store.** Did you know that in the old days, things were always sold in bulk, and people brought their own containers to the general store? Take a look at this photo: *en.wikipedia.org/wiki/ File:General_store_ interior_Alabama_ USA.jpg*

• **A site about garbage** from the U.S. government. You might need a grown-up to explain some of it: *eia.doe.gov/ kids/energyfacts/saving/ recycling/solidwaste/ primer.html*

• **It's a waste.** *www.epa.gov/epawaste/index.htm*

There's a lot more to see and do at **50simplekids.com**

5. PASS IT ON

Take a Guess:
How much of the stuff we throw out could be recycled?
A) None of it—garbage is no good for anything
B) Just a little bit   C) More than half of it

Wouldn't it be great if there was a way to help save the Earth, get rid of stuff you don't want, and make someone happy, all at the same time?

There is.

Instead of throwing away your old things, you can find a new home for them.

You know those old board games you don't play with any more...or that Dr. Seuss book you've outgrown ...or those easy puzzles you can do with your eyes closed? Try passing them on rather than tossing them out.

You'll be saving a little piece of our Earth. And someone might love them.

Did You Know

• Since the things you use are all made from materials that come from the Earth, they're still valuable, even when you don't need them anymore.

• By passing them on to other people instead of throwing

Answer: C. That's enough garbage to fill a football stadium from top to bottom every day!

them out, you make less garbage and save precious resources.

• Some groups, like the Salvation Army and Goodwill, collect used things to sell in stores.

• Used books are often collected by libraries for special book sales that raise money to buy new library books. And some "used book" stores will let you trade in your old books for credit to buy different ones!

• Old games and toys can often be donated to hospitals or other places where kids need something to play with.

What You Can Do

At Home

• Go through your closet, your attic, your basement…even look under your bed! Find the things that you don't want anymore, but someone else might love.

• Find places that can use your old things. Look in the phone book and write down the numbers for your local hospital, library, Salvation Army, and so on. Call them.

• Some recycling centers take clothes and books to pass on to others. They call it "freecycling." This means they recycle our old stuff by giving it away for free!

• Have a garage sale. Put up signs in your neighborhood that say "Garage Sale at (your address) from

9 AM to 5 PM on (the date)." Then put your old things out on the driveway or lawn, and put a price on each of them. People will buy what they want. Then you can give the rest of it away. It's a great way to make money and recycle at the same time.

At School

• Have a book swap. Make it a class project: Pick a day for people to bring in old books to trade.

• Sponsor a "Share Project." Collect used things from the community and distribute them, or sell them and use the money for a good cause your class picks.

See for Yourself

• **What's It Worth?** Tips about garage sales: *yardsalequeen.com*

• **Garage sale tips (read with a grown-up):** *thriftyfun.com/ tf54049630.tip.html* or *getrichslowly.org/blog/2007/06/12/ a-yard-sale-checklist-ten-tips-for-garage-sale-prep/*

• **Freecycle!** Check out *freecycle.com* for a different way to think about stuff. Also check out *freemesa.org*

6. USE IT AGAIN...AND AGAIN...AND AGAIN...

Take a Guess:
How many disposable razors will Americans throw away today?
A) 4,500   B) 45,000   C) 4,500,000

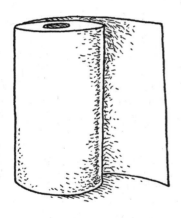

Long before you were born, back when your great-grandparents were kids, there was no such thing as a paper towel or a paper napkin. People used cloth. Back then, everything was used again and again. In fact, most people would never have imagined throwing something away after using it just once.

But today we have lots of things that are made especially to be tossed in the garbage after *one use*. We call them "disposable."

Aluminum foil, plastic bags, paper bags, plastic food wrap, and other products are all considered "disposable."

What's going on? Our Earth's treasures are being thrown out as trash. Wouldn't it be wonderful if everyone did a little something to stop this waste? Just imagine what a difference it would make!

Did You Know

• We use billions of feet of paper towels every year—and

Answer: C. Incredible!

about 3,000 tons of them *every day*. That's a lot of trees!

• Americans use nearly 55 million paper clips *every day*. That's about 20 billion a year!

• Americans buy and toss out 350 million disposable lighters and 2 billion plastic razors each year. That's millions of pounds of plastic made by factories just so grown-ups can throw it away!

What You Can Do

• Keep a cloth towel by the sink. Next time you rinse your hands or need to wipe up a spill, grab the cloth towel instead of a paper one.

• Save plastic bags and use them again. If they're dirty, turn them inside out, rinse them, and hang them up to dry.

• Aluminum foil is reusable, too. Wash it off, let it dry, and put it away. When it can't be used again, recycle it.

• Keep a "rag bag" handy. Put your old, torn clothes in it, and you'll have a supply of rags to help you out with messy chores or art projects.

• Make a scrap-paper pad. Gather some scrap paper that's all the same size (you may have to cut them). Stack 10 to 20 sheets, with the blank sides up. Staple them together at the top, and you're done, you've made a pad.

- Start a "Save-It" drawer—a place to keep useful, reuseable little items so you'll have them when you need them. If you don't have a drawer to use, then keep them in a little

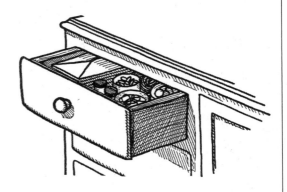

box or a plastic storage container. Collect paper clips, safety pins, pieces of string, rubber bands, and so on. Tell your family so they'll save and reuse them, too.

Amaze Your Friends

Take them on a *Disposable Treasure Hunt*. Search a house, a classroom, or the whole school for "disposable" things. Your friends will be fascinated to find out how many things we buy just to throw away.

Bonus: Ask them to try to picture where each thing comes from. Hold up a roll of paper towels and imagine it's a tree. Take a plastic bag or plastic wrap and try to see it as oil—or even better, a prehistoric creature. See aluminum foil as a precious metal from underground. They seem a lot more important now, don't they? They are!

See for Yourself

- **Watch this!** A video about reusing things, made by kids for kids: *youtube.com/watch?v=2Cs5bLu07t0*

- **"Here's my idea":** *kidshealthnotes.com/2008/04/22/recycle-with-kids-tip-5-reusing-beats-recycling/*

- **A checklist of reuseables:** *recycleworks.org/kids*

7. BE A RECYCLING DETECTIVE

Take a Guess:
Recycling centers can sometimes be found...
A) In supermarket parking lots B) On school playgrounds
C) At fire stations

I magine that you're a master detective. You have an important job: Your family wants to recycle everything they can...but they don't have enough information.

Where are the recycling centers in town? How many are there? What materials will they take?

These mysteries must be solved before anyone can recycle...and *you* can solve them!

How? Do a little detective work. Follow the clues, ask the right questions—and you'll come up with the answers.

For Recycling Detectives Only
Here are your Top 3 assignments:

Assignment #1: Find out if your town has curbside recycling.

• In many communities, trucks will pick up at least *some* recyclables at the curb in front of your home. This is called "curbside recycling." Do you have it in your neighborhood?

Assignment #2: Track down the nearest recycling centers.
• If you don't have curbside recycling, you need to find places to take your recyclables. And even if you *do* have

Answer: All of them.

curbside pickup, you may need to know where to bring other materials to be recycled.

Assignment #3: Get the facts about recyclables.

• Once you've found a recycler—whether it's a curbside program or a recycling center—you have to find out what materials they take and how they want materials prepared.

What You Can Do

• It should be pretty simple to find out if there's curbside recycling in your area. Ask your parents…your neighbors…your teachers…or the garbage collector.

• If no one seems to know, try calling city hall (where your city government is). Ask someone there.

• For the telephone number, either go online or look in the "Government" pages in the front of your phone book.

• To get the facts about local recycling centers, look in the yellow pages under "Recycling." Call the centers listed and ask: 1) Where are they, and how do you get there? 2) When are they open? 3) What materials do they take? and 4) Do materials need to be prepared or sorted in any special way?

• You might also ask whether they *pay* for some recyclables (like aluminum).

• Keep notes. As you learn things, write them down so you won't forget them. That way, you can share them with your family later.

• It's especially important to make a list of the materials that can be recycled in your community; that way, you'll have the information handy when you decide what to recycle at home or school.

• Now you're a recycling detective!

See for Yourself

• **Find a recycling center.** Just put in your zip code, and chances are, this web site will tell you where your local recycling centers are: *recyclingcenters.org*

• **Recycling and Beyond.** A few fun ways to learn. Try the game "It's not all garbage": *dnr.state.wi.us/org/caer/ce/ eek/earth/recycle/recyclingbeyond.htm*

• **Recycling Roundup.** *kids.nationalgeographic.com/Games/ ActionGames/Recycle-roundup*

• **Recycling Revolution.** Not as much fun, but it's got lots of information: *recycling-revolution.com*

8. THE NO-GARBAGE LUNCH

Take a Guess:
What's the best way to take a sandwich to school?
A) In your pocket   B) On a leash   C) In a reusable container

Lunchtime!
   What did you bring today? A sandwich…an apple…a package of cookies…
   Anything else?
   How about your brown paper lunch bag, your plastic sandwich bag, and the wrapper the cookies came in?

   All this packaging is part of your lunch, too. It's also part of our garbage problem, because when you're done, you throw it away.

   Want to stop this waste? Learn how to make a "no-garbage lunch."

Did You Know

• Lunchtime trash is the second-largest source of waste in U.S. schools. (Paper is #1.)

• If you bring a brown-bag lunch to school every day, you can create more than 65 pounds of waste by the end of the year. If everyone did it, that could be over *nine tons* of lunch waste…just for an average-size school!

• What are we throwing away? Well, every year Americans discard 380 billion plastic bags (that's about 1,200 plastic

Answer: C. A reusable container means a lot less garbage.

bags a person) and nearly 2.7 billion juice boxes. And that's just *two* of the things we turn into garbage.

What You Can Do

Take a no-garbage lunch to school. That's exactly what it sounds like—a lunch that leaves you with no (or very little) garbage to throw away when you're finished.

A few tips on making one:

1) Pick a no-garbage lunch carrier, *such as:*

• A brown paper bag. When you're done eating, save the bag so you can use it again the next day.

• A lunch box. It can last for years...and it will keep your lunch from getting squished!

• A reusable cloth lunch bag. Decorate it—be creative. Some decorating tips: *activitytv.com/597-reusable-lunch-bag*

2. Sandwiches

• Carry a sandwich or other food in a reusable container.

• Wrap your sandwich in aluminum foil. Foil can be washed off and reused. It can also be recycled.

• Use a "zip-lock" plastic bag. It's easy to rinse and reuse.

• Food tip: If you cut a sandwich in quarters, it can fit inside any container.

3. Snacks

• Buy snacks in large packages instead of small individual ones—you get more food and less packaging for your money. For example, instead of buying lots of little bags of pretzels, buy one big bag. Then bring the pretzels to school each day in a reusable container.

• Pick snacks that come in their own natural wrappers, like bananas and oranges. If you have a compost pile, save the peels and compost them (see Simple Thing #9).

4. Drinks

• Try carrying your milk or juice in a small thermos.

• Buy drinks that come in recyclable containers.

See for Yourself

• **Success stories!** Wonderful ideas about working with these programs at school: *wastefreelunches.org/success.html*

• **Cool reusables!** Reusable lunch items that look cool: *reusablebags.com/store/wrapnmat-p-2.html*

• **Lunch box language.** The ultimate web site of old lunchboxes and their history: *lunchboxpad.com*

• **Crochet a lunch bag out of recycled materials!** If someone can teach you to crochet, it's a great way to recycle: *marloscrochetcorner.com/ Plastic%20Bag%20tote.html*

9. MAKE NEW DIRT

Take a Guess:
Which of these is something worms won't eat?
A) A juicy steak   B) Fruit   C) Vegetables

When you're done with your dinner, is there still a little food left on your plate? What are you going to do with it? This may sound strange, but you don't have to throw it away. You can save it, and turn it back into rich, fertile soil—one of the Earth's greatest treasures. Then you can use it for growing plants.

This is called *composting*. It's so simple, anyone can do it.

Did You Know

• You can make compost with leaves and grass clippings, or food scraps. Most garbage that's organic—which means "made out of things that were once alive"—will work.

• Boy, do we have plenty of organic garbage to use! More than half of the trash your family throws away every year is organic.

• In fact, every year each of us tosses out about 1,200 pounds of organic garbage!

• How much is that? Well, if you weigh 100 pounds, then the organic garbage you throw away in a year weighs about 12 times more than you do!

• If we composted that garbage instead of throwing it away, we'd be making new dirt that's great to grow things in!

Answer: A. Worms won't eat meat.

What You Can Do

There are many easy ways to compost.

- **By yourself.** The simplest way is to make a pile of leaves and grass clippings in a corner of your yard. In a while, the pile will turn into soil.

- **With an adult.** Build a special bin for compost and put organic garbage in it. Turn it over every once in a while, and watch it slowly become a part of the Earth again. Check out some of the web sites listed on the next page for details about what foods work best, and other info.

- **At school.** Every school has a lot of food waste from the cafeteria and lunches. Most of it gets thrown away. But lots of schools around the U.S. are starting to give composting a try. The Mansfield Middle School, in Mansfield, Connecticut, even has a web site to show other schools how to do it. Check it out: *mansfieldct.org/schools/mms/compost/*

Amaze Your Friends

Tell them that the most interesting way to compost is with worms. Worms? Believe it or not, they're great composters! They eat rotting food, and poop out rich soil. No kidding!

Here's how you compost with worms:

1) Build a wooden box about two feet wide, two feet long, and eight inches deep.

2) Fill the box with moist bedding like shredded paper or leaves.

3) Buy some red worms at a local nursery (or maybe a bait shop) and put them in.

4) Add one pound of worms for every half-pound of food to start. They will multiply quickly.

5) Put in two handfuls of soil. You can put in household food waste—except for meat, bones, dairy products, fatty food, or any "hard-to-digest" materials such as avocado pits. Mix them into the box, and then stand back!

See for Yourself

• **Compost anywhere!** *kidsregen.org/krrn/10_step/step3/detective.shtml*

• **It's Wiggly Worm:** *youtube.com/watch?v=kq3yfKCC9ok*

• **Composting with the Greens:** *meetthegreens.pbskids.org /episode4/kitchen-composting.html* and *meetthegreens.pbskids. org/episode4/outdoor-composting.html*

• **A composting slide show:** *sustainable.tamu.edu/slidesets/ kidscompost/cover.html*

• **Make a worm bin!** *kidsgardening.org/growonder/worm.php*

• **For teachers and parents:** *www.gardeners.com/Kids-and-Composting/5329,default,pg.html*

More to see and do at **50simplekids.com**

PRESERVING
OUR
OCEANS,

RIVERS,
LAKES, AND
STREAMS

WATER THOUGHTS

Take a minute and try to imagine a day without water. It makes you realize just how precious water is, doesn't it?

Here's something else to think about: Each year there are more and more people living on the Earth, but the amount of water stays the same. This means that there is less water to go around: less water for each person; less water for plants; less water for other animals.

And yet, we keep wasting it!

For a long time it seemed as though there was so much water, it didn't matter how we used it. Now we know better…and we know that it's time to try something new!

So in this section you'll find plenty of easy ways to conserve water, to protect our streams, lakes, and rivers, and even help save our oceans.

By being a leak detective, by cleaning beaches and streams, by paying attention to showers and faucets, and by trying out the other Simple Things included here, you can have a positive impact on our water supply . . . and you can have a lot of fun doing it!

10. BE A WATER-LEAK DETECTIVE

Take a Guess:
If a leaky faucet fills a coffee cup in 10 minutes, how much water will it waste in a year? Enough for:
A) A glass of water   B) A bath   C) 52 baths

Calling all kids! Calling all kids! Be on the lookout for hidden water leaks in your house. Secret hiding places include: Behind the walls, in faucets, in toilets...and even outside, at the end of a hose.

Your mission as a water-leak detective is to find the hidden leaks ... and help stop them!

Did You Know

• Even a tiny leak can waste a lot of water. For example, a leak that fills up a coffee cup in 10 minutes will waste over 3,000 gallons of water in a year.

• How much water is that? You'd have to drink 65 glasses of water every day *for a year* to get that much water!

• The average U.S. home loses 22 gallons of water every day just because of leaks!

• The biggest leakers are faucets and toilets. About 20% of all the toilets in American homes are leaking right now...and most people don't even know it. Is yours?

Answer: C. Enough to take 52 baths...one for every week of the year!

What You Can Do

At Home

• Find out if there's a leak! First, get a parent to teach you how to read the water meter. If you have a meter, it will probably be in the corner of your basement, on the outside wall of your house, or next to the street, under a cement or metal cover.

• Then pick a time when everyone is going to be out of the house, and no one will be using the water—when the whole family is about to go out shopping or to a movie, for example.

• Before you leave, read the water meter and write down its setting. Then when you get back home, take another reading. If the numbers have changed, you've probably discovered a leak! Tell your parents what you've found.

At School

• Help find leaks like some students at Homestead-Wakefield Elementary School in Bel Air, Maryland, did.

According to news reports, they "measured and analyzed how much water was being wasted by leaky faucets in their school."

• Then they wrote letters explaining the problem and asked the staff to help them come up with a solution.

• You can do it, too. Talk to your teacher about setting up a leak patrol to find leaky faucets, toilets, and outdoor hoses.

Amaze Your Friends

Show them how easy it is to check their toilets for leaks. Here's how:

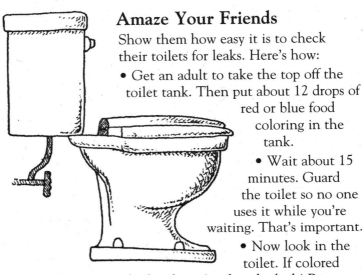

- Get an adult to take the top off the toilet tank. Then put about 12 drops of red or blue food coloring in the tank.

- Wait about 15 minutes. Guard the toilet so no one uses it while you're waiting. That's important.

- Now look in the toilet. If colored water shows up in the bowl, you've found a leak! Be sure to tell someone about it. You'll save water...*and money!*

See for Yourself

- **Bert & Phil's Water Busters Game:** *www2.seattle.gov/util/waterbusters/*

- **Help Bert and Phil fix leaks** and conserve water around the house! *www.savingwater.org/kids*

- **And here are Bert's tips on saving water** inside and outside your house (Share them with your parents): *dnr.metrokc.gov/wtd/waterconservation/tips.htm*

- **The Meter Reading Game.** Practice reading the water meter. You might need some help figuring out the numbers: *http://greeleygov.com/Water/Documents/metergame.swf*

- **Water fun!** *dcwasa.com/kids/index.html*

- **See what other kids do:** *pbskids.org/eekoworld/exchange/detail_water.html?Start=140*

11. PRESTO, ON!
PRESTO, OFF!

Take a Guess:

You can save up to 20,000 gallons of water a year by not letting the water run when you don't need it. That's enough to fill:
A) *A garbage can* **B)** *A big truck* **C)** *A swimming pool*

Imagine pumping water or hauling it from a well every time you wanted to brush your teeth, like they used to in the old days. It was hard work!

Life is easier now. We can just turn on a faucet and…presto…water! In fact, it's so easy to get water that we let gallons of it go down the drain without thinking!

We need a little water-saving magic: Presto, on!…Presto, off! Don't go with the flow!

Did You Know

• Water comes out of the faucet faster than you think. For example: while you're waiting for water to get cold enough to have a drink, you could fill six half-gallon milk cartons!

• If you leave the water running while you brush your teeth, you can waste five gallons of water. That's enough to fill 53 cans of soda!

• If you use a pail of water and a sponge to wash your family car instead of using the hose (except to rinse), you can save up to 150 gallons of water!

Answer: C. You save enough water to fill a swimming pool.

What You Can Do

• When you brush your teeth: Just wet your brush, then turn off the water...and then turn it on again when you need to rinse your brush off. You'll save up to nine gallons of water each time! That's enough to give your pet a bath.

• When you're thirsty: If you like cool water, why not leave a bottle of it in the refrigerator instead of letting the water run? You'll save water and still have a cool drink.

• When you wash dishes by hand: If you just fill up the basin and rinse dishes in it, instead of letting the water run, you can save up to 25 gallons each time. That's enough to take a 5 to 10-minute shower.

• When you're going to take a bath: Plug the tub before you let the water run, so you don't waste any.

• When you wash your hands: Turn the water off while you're using the soap. Then turn it back on to rinse.

Amaze Your Friends

See how much water we really use

• Ask them to guess how long it takes to fill a half-gallon milk carton with water. 30 seconds? A minute?

• Now demonstrate: Get an empty half-gallon milk carton, open it, and hold it under the faucet. Turn on the faucet and time it.

• How long did it take to fill the carton? Imagine that all over the U.S., people are letting the water run like that. Don't be one of them!

P.S.—Don't waste that water by pouring it down the sink. Pour it on a thirsty plant instead. Good work.

See for Yourself

• **Watch these short ads** made by high school kids: *usewaterwisely.com/videowinners.cfm*

• **Water-saving tips for kids, by kids!** *harwichwater.com/ resources/conservation/conservation_06.html*

• **10 tips to save water.** Share these with your family: *ajc.com/metro/content/metro/stories/2007/10/25/wateruse_ 1026.html*

• **Water-saving at school.** Save with the Lindfield East Public School in Australia: *schools.nsw.edu.au/events/state competitions/webawards/winners2006/primary/6/index.htm*

• **Take a family water audit.** An easy quiz, plus 100 ways to save water: *wateruseitwisely.com/familywater/index.shtml*

• **Down the Drain**—A water-saving program your teacher will want to know about! Work with students from around the world: *k12science.org/curriculum/drainproj/index.html*

12. SEE YOU AT THE BEACH

Take a Guess:
What are you most likely to find on a beach?
A) Monsters B) Sand castles C) Lots of garbage

Flash! Warning! Flash! Warning! We need help! Our beaches are in trouble. There's garbage in the ocean. There's litter on the beach.

This is serious. Lots of animals live in the ocean. And we can't live without healthy oceans, either. We get most of our air, moisture, and even our weather from them.

But what can one kid do? You can't save the whole ocean by yourself…but you *can* help to save a little piece of it. Here are some things to think about next time you go to the beach.

Did You Know

• Plastic bags and other plastic garbage thrown into the ocean kill more than one million sea creatures every year!

• Some of the garbage in the ocean comes from boats or ships. But most of it comes from beaches, or from garbage that spills into rivers and flows into the ocean.

• Plastic floating in the sea often looks like food to ocean animals. For example: Plastic bags look like jellyfish to sea turtles, which swallow them…and then die.

Answer: C. Unfortunately, people forget that animals live on the beach.

• Birds also get in trouble. They sometimes mistake little bits of plastic for food and choke on them.

• So you might save an animal's life just by picking up plastic from a beach.

What You Can Do

• Don't throw any kind of litter on the beach.

• When you visit the beach, take along a large garbage bag. Try to fill it with trash, close it tightly, then throw it in a garbage can. (If there are none on the beach, take the bag with you.)

• If you find any bottles or aluminum cans on the beach, bring them home for recycling. (But don't pick up broken glass!)

• If you go fishing, never throw fishing line in the water—birds and sea creatures get tangled in it and die.

• Join the crowd! Every year, there's a big beach cleanup all over the world. People get together and patrol beaches in their area for three hours. They pick up millions of pounds of garbage and save many animals. Does that sound like fun? Check out *www.oceanconservancy.org* and click on "Coastal Cleanup."

Amaze Your Friends

• Tell them about the *Trash Vortex* (also called the *Pacific Garbage Patch*), a gigantic plastic soup that moves around the ocean like "a big animal without a leash."

• This is a real thing, found in the 1990s by a sea captain named Charles Moore. He says: "There were shampoo caps and soap bottles and plastic bags and fishing floats as far as I could see. Here I was in the middle of the ocean, and there was nowhere I could go to avoid the plastic."

• Bad news: The Vortex is getting bigger all the time! Right now it is twice as big as the state of Texas (look at a map of the USA, and find Texas. That's BIG!) It's more than 1,000 miles long!

• Want to learn more? Get your teacher or parents to help you read about the Algalita Marine Research Center: *algalita.org/index.html*

See for Yourself

• **Be an Ocean Guardian (a pdf to print out):** *sanctuaries.noaa.gov/education/pdfs/ogab.pdf*

• **Thank you, ocean!** *thankyouocean.org/for_kids*

• **Tell your teachers.** They can find student handouts about plastics in the ocean, and what we can do at: *www.algalita.org/plastics-in-the-environment.html*

13. SHOWER POWER

Take a Guess:
How many milk cartons can you fill with the
water from a five-minute shower?
A) 5   B) 10   C) 50

What if you turned on the faucet and no water came out? We need to save water now, so that will never happen!

One thing you can do is check to see if your shower is using too much water. There's an easy test you can do to find out. It's on page 63.

Did You Know

• When you shower, you can use five gallons of water every minute! How much water is that? Enough to fill 50 big glasses!

• A whole shower can easily take 10 minutes. So every day, you could use 50 gallons of water taking one shower.

• In a year, that's almost 20,000 gallons for your showers!

• Taking a bath generally uses even more water than showers—up to twice as much.

• Shower secret: Your family can put in a special "low-flow" shower head. This adds air to the water, so it cuts the amount of water used from five gallons a minute to as little as one or two! But you don't even notice it—it still feels great!

Answer: C. Think how high 50 milk cartons stacked on top of each other would reach!

What You Can Do

• Take showers instead of baths. Or fill the tub up only halfway. This saves water right away. One bonus: Singing in a shower sounds better than singing in a bath.

• Take shorter showers. For every minute you cut, you could save five gallons of water. So if you take a five-minute shower, you could save 25 gallons of water!

• Time yourself. Use any kind of alarm clock or kitchen timer...or ask someone to buy a *shower-timer* to help you keep track. (Check it out: *zwello.com/rip-dt-duck.html*)

• Tell your parents about "low-flow" shower heads. You can find them at most hardware stores. Here's how to understand what they do: The water flow of a shower is measured in *gallons per minute* (gpm). That tells you how many gallons of water the shower puts out in one minute.

• So, if a showerhead flows at 2 gpm, you're using only 10 gallons in a five-minute shower. The old 5-gpm showerheads would use about 25 gallons—a *big* difference!

Amaze Your Friends

Tell them about the World-Famous Showerhead Milk Carton Test:

• You need an empty milk carton, a watch with a second-hand, and an adult to time you.

• Open the top of the milk carton so it forms a square.

• Turn on the water so it's a normal shower flow. Then get in (not with your clothes on, of course) and hold the milk carton up to the shower head for 10 seconds. The adult with the watch should tell you when to start and when time is up.

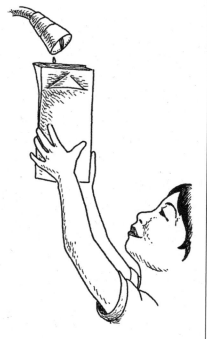

• If the carton overflows in less than 10 seconds, your showerhead uses too much water. It's that simple!

See for Yourself

• **What's your shower power?** Compare the water you use with other kids' use: *pbskids.org/zoom/activities/sci/ showerestimation.html*

• **Save for the Future.** A cartoon that reminds us why we're doing all this: *youtube.com/watch?v= INhlh8MtDZI&feature=related*

• **Hip shower tip:** *youtube.com/watch?v=dyLj36nXgwQ*

• **Watch with parents:** *youtube.com/watch?v=21OBHk5-0UU*

There's a lot more to see and do at **50simplekids.com**

14. DON'T DUMP IT!

Take a Guess:
Which of these would you want in your drinking water?
A) Furniture polish   B) Paint thinner   C) Motor oil

If you dug a hole as far as you could go, would you ever reach China? Of course not. But you *would* reach water! Underground, there's lots of fresh water. We need to take care of it to keep it clean for all living things.

How can you take care of something underground?

Simple—just make sure nothing harmful is spilled on the ground that will soak down into our water!

Did You Know

• Most of the water in the world isn't drinkable!

• The oceans cover 2/3 of the Earth, but ocean water is salty, so no one can drink it.

Answer: None, of course. But if we don't dispose of them properly, they end up in our water!

• There's a lot of water in the polar ice caps, but we can't drink ice. Hmm-m-m. Well, actually, global warming is starting to melt that ice—but it's becoming part of the salty ocean, so we're losing *that* drinking water, too!

• What's left to drink? The freshwater in lakes, rivers, and streams…and *groundwater*—water sitting underground in layers of sand and rock. That's where our wells come from.

• It's really easy to pollute groundwater. Just dumping common, everyday things on the ground can do it, because the Earth is like a sponge that soaks everything in.

• For example, a gallon of paint or a quart of motor oil can seep into the Earth and pollute 250,000 gallons of drinking water. And a spilled gallon of gasoline can pollute 750,000 gallons of water!

What You Can Do

• Be careful about what you spill on the Earth. You can't avoid accidents, but don't dump harmful liquids onto the ground on purpose.

• When you're not sure what to do with a can of oil, paint, or gasoline, bring it to an adult. *Don't* throw it away! It should be saved for a special garbage pickup called "toxic waste collection." You probably won't be using much paint, motor oil, or gasoline soon… but it's not too early to start thinking about this.

Amaze Your Friends

Make Your Own Aquifer

• Underground supplies of water are called *aquifers*. You and your friends can't go down there to look at them, but you can build your own aquifer. (It's a great school project, too.) Instructions are here: *mcwa.com/kids.htm#cycle*

• But, come to think of it, why make an aquifer from sand when you can make an Edible Aquifer from chocolate, vanilla ice cream, and soda! Find it here: *www.dnr.state.wi.us/org/caer/ce/eek/cool/ameliaedibleaquifer.htm*

See for Yourself

• **Groundwater.org** has information for you, your parents, and your teachers: *groundwater.org/kc/kc.html*

• **Musical groundwater video:** *groundwater.org/kc/groundwater_animation.html*

• **Interactive animations from Texas!** Check out "The Water Cycle" and "Groundwater": *twdb.state.tx.us/kids/*

• **Be the judge** of the water cycle in Science Court: *tomsnyder.com/products/productextras/SCISCI/watercycle.html*

• **Play Droplet & The Water Cycle** (like Pacman for water drops!): *kids.earth.nasa.gov/droplet.html*

15. CATCH SOME RUNNING WATER

Take a Guess:
What's the best way to sweep a driveway or patio clean?
A) A broom   B) A water hose   C) An anteater

Next time there's a rainstorm, go outside and watch all the water flowing off your walkway, your roof, and your driveway.

That water is called *runoff*. As it washes down the street, rolling toward the sewer (or *storm drain*), it picks up a lot of gross stuff: oil, chemicals, garbage, dirt. Ugh!

Keep watching: The water finally reaches the storm drain and, whoosh!—it disappears into the grate. It's gone!... But where did it go?

Well, the runoff goes into big underground pipes and flows *right into* our streams and rivers. So all the poisons and pollutants it picks up on the street go directly into our waterways, too!

That's why polluted runoff is *the #1 source of water pollution* in the United States!

Do you want to help protect our freshwater? You can do it by catching runoff *before* it leaves your yard.

Answer: A. A broom! But too many people use a hose and waste lots of precious water.

Did You Know

• The reason stormwater runoff is such a problem? We've covered so much of the Earth with tar and concrete.

• Normally, rainwater lands on the Earth and slowly seeps into the ground. Pollutants get filtered out, and it becomes pure drinking water in underground *aquifers*.

• But now roads, driveways, roofs, and parking lots don't let the water get to the Earth. Instead, it becomes runoff.

• In cities, almost half of all surfaces are paved. So a typical city block has *nine times more runoff* than woodlands.

• In addition to water pollution, storm-water runoff causes flooding and erosion that washes out streams and river-banks.

What You Can Do

At Home

• Get your family to put in a rain barrel that catches water from your roof. (See next page for details.)

• Sweep your driveway, don't hose it off. The same goes for sidewalks and gutters.

• Don't litter. One rain shower will wash plastic bags and other lit-ter, including cigarette butts (eeww!), down the storm drain and into our waterways.

• When your family washes the car, do it on the lawn or at a commercial car wash—not in the driveway or street. Use a bucket and sponge instead of a hose.

At School
Start a Storm Drain Ranger program at your school, like they

have in San Francisco. Check out their program here: *kidsforthebay.org/programs/stormdrainrangers.htm*

Amaze Your Friends

• Show them the web sites for rain barrels. A rain barrel is a big container that catches rainwater from your roof instead of letting it run off. Then you can use the water on your lawn or garden, or to wash your car.

• A rain barrel can be made from a large plastic trash can or a wood barrel. Check these sites out with a parent or teacher: *rainbarrelguide.com*. Or this pdf: *www.conserve watergeorgia.net/resources/Rain_Barrel_Construction_ Handout.pdf*

See for Yourself

• **Games and puzzles** from the Stormwater Coalition: *stormwatercoalition.org/html/playhouse/index.html*

• **Join a raindrop** on a trip through polluted runoff: *www.twdb.state.tx.us/kids/modules/rain_journey/index.html*

• **Meet Secret Agent Worms:** *secretagentworms.org/vault_ stormwater.html*

16. THE LAWN RANGER

Take a Guess:
When grass is tall, it…
A) Explodes   B) Has deeper roots   C) Plays basketball

D o you water the lawn at your house? A lot of kids get that job during summer. If you're one of them, here are some water-saving tips for you.

Did You Know

• In the summertime, Americans use about 1/3 more water than we do the rest of the year. Why? Because we're watering our lawns.

• There are over 30 million acres of lawns in the U.S. To water that much grass, we need *270 billion gallons* of water every week! That's enough to give every person in the world a shower four days in a row!

• Some people think that the more you water your lawn, the better it is. But that's not true. Most lawns are watered twice as much as they need to be. This means that with the water many people now use on their lawns, they could actually water two lawns. What a huge waste of water!

• Actually, most lawns only need *one inch* of water per week.

What You Can Do

• Water only early in the morning or in the evening, when the chances of the water drying up in the heat—that's called *evaporation*—are the lowest.

• Don't water on windy days. The wind blows water away.

Answer: B. Taller grass has deeper roots, and is more likely to survive.

• Make sure your sprinklers are watering the lawn and not the sidewalk or driveway.

• Use a watering can or hose for small areas that need more water. Be sure to water slowly and deeply, so the roots that need the water the most are able to get it.

Amaze Your Friends

• Show them the "inch test." This is a simple test that tells you how long your sprinkler should be on. You'll need a ruler, a watch, and three cans that are the same size.

• Set the cans on your lawn. One should be close to the sprinkler, one should be medium distance away, and the last should be at the far end of the sprinkler's reach.

• Now turn on the sprinkler. Check every few minutes and see how long it takes for an inch of water to build up in each can. Write down how long it takes for each one.

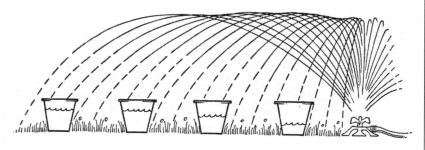

• Now add the three times together and divide by three to get an average time. (You may need an older sister or brother or an adult, to help you with the math.)

• The number you get is the amount of time you need to water your lawn for it to get an inch of water. If you water the lawn that long each week, it will get the water it needs, but not too much.

See for Yourself

Watering and planting needs are different, depending on what part of the country you live in.

• **Find the right way** to water where *you* live—contact the water or parks department of your town and ask them if an inch a week is the right amount where you live.

• **Or if there's a state university near you,** they might have a "Cooperative Extension" program that has lots of info and tips about native plants and grasses. Find one close to you at: *csrees.usda.gov/Extension*

• **Watch this!** It's a video about the best way to water your lawn: *youtube.com/watch?v=O818bjcu6LI*

• **And this!** Another video about watering your lawn with the environment in mind: *youtube.com/watch?v=D61XUBCvjNI*

• **Garden Girl speaks up** for edible gardens: *youtube.com/watch?v=X_4LMoaCVFA&feature=related*

• **Native plants.** One way people are using less water on their lawns is by making their lawns smaller. Instead of grass, they plant something called native plants. Check out: *wildflower.org/*

• **Schools like native plants!** Here's a school project: *kidsgardening.com/themes/native2.asp*

There's a lot more to see and do at **50simplekids.com**

17. ADOPT A STREAM

Take a Guess:
Which of these would you probably find in a stream?
A) Fish   B) Old tires   C) Pebbles

Streams and creeks are great places to play. They're fun to explore, wade in, skip rocks in...they're even fun to listen to. And if you stay very quiet awhile, you may see some birds or other animals—because they depend on streams, too.

Unfortunately, lots of streams have become polluted or filled with garbage. Someone needs to help make them clean again. How about it? You and your friends can help take care of the Earth by adopting a stream in your area.

Did You Know

• The color and smell of a stream can tell you a lot about what's happening to it.

• **Green water:** Can mean very small plants called algae are in the water. This makes it hard for any other life to exist in the stream.

• **Muddy water:** Can mean there's too much dirt in the water, which makes it hard for fish to breathe.

Answer: You'd find all of them. Fish and pebbles belong in streams, but old tires don't!

The stream may need more plants along its banks.

- **A shiny film on the water:** Can mean there's oil leaking into the stream. That's poison, and it should be stopped.

- **Foam in the water:** Can mean soap from homes or factories is leaking in.

- **Rotten egg smell:** Bad news! Sewage could be leaking into the stream! Sewage carries germs that can make us very sick and kill stream life.

- **Orange or red coating on the water:** Might mean a factory is dumping pollutants into the stream.

- If you find fish or lots of bugs in the water, that's a good sign. It means there's a lot of oxygen there.

What You Can Do

- Patrol the stream bank and pick up all the trash you can find. Make sure you put it in a trash can, or bring a garbage bag with you and take it back to your house to throw away.

- Try not to let your pet leave its waste in or near a stream. Animal waste can pollute the water in a stream.

- If you find anything like oil or sewage leaking into the water, report it to a parent or other adult.

At School

"Adopt" a creek: Join a clean-up program, or start your own.

• For example: During the annual "Creek Week" in Santa Barbara, California, 500 volunteers—including schoolkids—planted native plants and trees, and cleaned out over a ton of trash and weeds at Sycamore Creek. Then, as part of an after-school program, Franklin Elementary School students made weekly trips to the creek to care for the plants. What can *your* class do?

Amaze Your Friends

• Show them how to make a "Litter Skimmer," a cool contraption that cleans garbage out of a stream *all by itself*!

• See these sites:
1) *fosc.org/Wheaton BrCleanup2005.htm*

2) *50simplethings.com/ litterskimmer*

See for Yourself

• **Get dozens of great stories!** Just type *schools clean up creek* into a Google search.

• **The Izaak Walton League:** *iwla.org/*

• **Watch this video:** *worldinvestigators.blogspot.com/ 2007/04/river-clean-up-07.html*

18. PROTECT OUR WETLANDS

Take a Guess:
What kind of animals live in wetlands?
A) Frogs   B) Dinosaurs   C) Gorillas

Have you ever been to a swamp, a bog, or a marsh? They're muddy, messy, and wet, and sometimes they *really* stink!

But here's a surprise: These *wetlands* are also some of the most important places on Earth.

They're home to thousands of different kinds of living things. Birds, fish, frogs, and other animals depend on them…and many plants, like cattails, grow *only* in wetlands.

On top of all that, wetlands play a big part in keeping our water clean and controlling floods.

The bad news is that we've been destroying our wetlands. We've filled them full of dirt to build houses and factories. We've put roads where they used to be. We've drained them and planted crops there.

When we lose wetlands, we lose the good things they do for us…and we lose the living things that need them. That's why it's so important to take action now, and save them.

Did You Know

• Native American Indians called wetlands the "between-lands," because they are not really land and they are not really water. They are "where the water meets the land."

• Healthy wetlands support more different kinds of life than any other natural habitat.

• *All* species of freshwater fish depend on them, and about half of our bird species live or feed there. About half of our endangered species depend on them, too.

• Yet in the last 300 years, over half of America's wetlands have been drained, filled in, or paved over. And every day, we lose more of them.

What You Can Do

• Celebrate American Wetlands Month in May. It's a great way to "get your feet wet" with wetlands projects. Check out: *www.epa.gov/owow/wetlands/awm/*

• Join Ducks Unlimited Greenwings. A $10 annual membership gets you copies of *Puddler* magazine, decals, and lots of games and activities. Plus, you join a group that is dedicated to protecting wetlands: *greenwing.org/index.html*

• Volunteer to work on a wetlands with friends, family, or your class. Get-your-hands-dirty "restoration" projects are really fun—planting, digging, and so forth. To find a wetlands in your area, get someone to help you contact a local environmental group, your parks department, or your state's natural resources department. You can take it from there.

Amaze Your Friends

Organize a Wetlands Field Trip

Show them how cool wetlands are and how much is going on there. You'll need a local map, a camera or a journal and pen, a plant identification guide for your area...and an adult! Get instructions for setting up a tour in the Wetlands section of our web site, *50simplekids.com*

See for Yourself

• **The basics:**
www.ag.iastate.edu/centers/iawetlands/About.html

• **Watch this!** Three videos about wetlands: *idahoptv.org/dialogue4kids/season6/wetlands/index.cfm*

• **PBS TV:** *pbskids.org/dragonflytv/show/wetlands.html*

• **Build wetlands at your school!**
kidsgardening.com/2005.kids.garden.news/october/pg1.html

• **Build wetlands in a pan.** You might need adult help: *swfwmd.state.fl.us/education/splash/building_a_wetland.html*

• **"My Wetlands Coloring Book"** (a pdf to print out):
americaswetland.com/files/MyWetlandsColoringBook.pdf

PROTECTING

ANIMALS

WILD
THOUGHTS

Why should we bother taking care of animals?

You probably wouldn't even ask such a silly question.
Kids understand why animals are important better than
grown-ups do.

But it's still a good question to think about.

Here's one reason: Every creature on the Earth deserves
to have a good life. And sometimes we can help.

Here's another reason: Every animal is part of the
beautiful chain of nature that exists on our Earth. The
littlest insect is as important to the survival of all life
on the planet as the biggest elephant or the smartest
person. All of us have a special place in the world.

What happens if one kind of animal disappears? Maybe
nothing we can notice...but something changes on our
Earth.

It makes sense to protect all animals. And it feels good.
And on top of that, it's fun.

19. FOR THE BIRDS

Take a Guess:
What is a hummingbird's favorite food?
A) Hot oatmeal   B) Sweet syrup   C) Twinkies

Splash! Ruffle! Splash! Have you ever watched a bird take a bath? It dips in, fluffs itself up, shakes all over, flaps its wings, and dips and flaps some more...and it looks like it's having the greatest time. It probably is!

That's why there are so many birds in yards with bird-baths. Setting up a bath or feeder is a great way to bring birds into your yard.

And when you do, you not only get to enjoy the birds, you also get to help the Earth.

Did You Know

• Birds are always hungry! They use up so much energy that they need to eat all the time.

• Sometimes birds eat 4/5 of their own weight in one day!

• What does that mean? Let's say you weigh 100 pounds. If you were a bird, you would have to eat 80 pounds of food between the time you woke up in the morning and the time you went to sleep at night! You can't do it! But birds can.

- Birds need water to drink (especially in summer) and to keep clean. They can have from about 1,000 to 25,000 feathers!...So they've got a lot of washing to do!

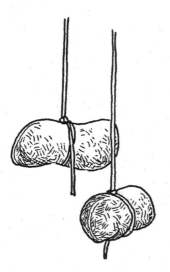

What You Can Do

Feed Some Birds at Home

- Make a bird feeder out of peanuts! Take a bunch of unsalted peanuts still in their shells, and tie them on a piece of yarn or string. Hang the string from a branch: birds will find it.

- Another nutty idea: Spread peanut butter all over a pinecone. Be sure to fill up all the little spaces. Then dip the pinecone in birdseed and hang it outside. Lots of birds like peanut butter.

- Hang some orange peels from trees—a great bird snack!

Make a Birdbath

- Find a ceramic or plastic saucer like the kind under potted plants. (Don't use metal. It will get too hot in the summer and freeze in the winter.) It should have some kind of edge around it for birds to rest on.

- Birds don't need the water to be too deep—about two inches is perfect. Keep the bath filled with water.

- If there are cats in the neighborhood, you probably need to put the birdbath up high or hang it from a tree.

Feed Birds at School

• Make and hang bird feeders to learn about local birds, like Project Feeder Watch at Sutherland Elementary in Palm Harbor, Florida.

• The kids hang their bird feeders in the schoolyard and then keep a scrapbook of the different birds they see.

• They also join the Cornell-Audubon Great Backyard Bird Count. Each counts birds with their families, then draws pictures and writes stories about the experience: *audubon.org/gbbc/index.shtml*

Amaze Your Friends

Give them three easy ways to help birds:

1. Put some dead branches or logs in their yards. Birds will live in dead trees and logs, and feed on the insects there.

2. Break ice on puddles in winter so birds can get a drink.

3. Save some of the soft hair from combing their dogs, and put it under the trees in their yard, or in a park. Nest-building birds can use it to give baby birds a soft mattress!

See for Yourself

• **Bird feeders!** Lots of homemade bird feeders: *a-home-for-wild-birds.com/bird-watching-for-kids.html*

• **More ideas.** Tips on how to create a bird habitat in your backyard: *pleasebekind.com/wild.html*

• **Bird facts and games.** From the National Zoo: *nationalzoo.si.edu/Animals/Birds/ForKids/*

• **The National Audubon Society.** The oldest bird protection group in the U.S.: *audubon.org/educate/*

20. IN YOUR OWN BACKYARD

Take a Guess:
What will a red currant bush attract to your backyard?
A) Space creatures   B) Butterflies   C) Grizzly bears

Where do wild animals live?
In the jungle? Yes.
In the forest? Uh-huh.
In the desert? You bet.

But guess what—they also live in cities, in suburbs, in backyards.

Wild animals? Yes!

Squirrels, birds, butterflies, and lots of other creatures live right near people. They're all part of the wild, wonderful Earth. And you can help them.

Did You Know

• Planting flowers, trees, or shrubs is a great way to give animals food and shelter in your own backyard.

• For example: You can attract butterflies with brightly colored flowers.

• Hummingbirds love red flowers.

Answer: B. You can create a home for animals just by planting the right bush or plant.

- Bats and moths like sweet-smelling white flowers.

- Some flowers, called *annuals*, are great for attracting birds. Why? Because they have lots of seeds...and you know how birds love seeds! Sunflowers, zinnias, and asters are annuals.

What You Can Do
At Home

- You and your family can design and plant a backyard garden—or a window box—that will attract animals.

- Check with a nursery or garden center to find out what kinds of plants will provide food and cover for your animal "neighbors."

- Or...make your backyard an official Wildlife Habitat. The National Wildlife Federation (NWF) will help you create a wild backyard. Then they'll certify your yard and offer a beautiful yard sign to tell your neighbors what you've done! Check out: *nwf.org/backyard*

At School

- Butterfly gardens are especially fun. All you need are the right plants and a good source of water...and butterflies will come. How many? Well, that depends on what you plant.

- For example: At Endeavor Elementary in Orlando, Florida, the kids picked plants that attract *12 kinds* of butterflies!

- On the other hand, the garden at Los Cerritos School in Paramount, California was specially planted to attract one type—*monarch* butterflies. It worked! Now monarchs stop at the school every year as they fly south toward Mexico.

- So...think about it. What kind of butterflies would be fun for *your* school?

Amaze Your Friends

• Build a hummingbird feeder and bring the birds to your yard or school garden. No bird species is more fun to watch—and they're easy to attract. (You'll need adult help for this project.)

• For instructions and recipes:

—*ehow.com/how_2243342_ hummingbird-feeder.html* or

—*fs.fed.us/wildflowers/ kids/activities/documents/ RecycledPlasticFeeders.pdf*

See for Yourself

• **Hummingbird info** with a great recipe for hummingbird food: *wildbirdshop.com/Birding/humfeed.html*

• **Kids' butterfly site.** You'll really like the pictures, stories and more: *kidsbutterfly.org*

• **Wildlife gardens:** *nwf.org/backyard/tipsheets.cfm*

• **Growonder** is an "e-magazine" with lots of fun gardening and outdoor projects: *kidsgardening.org/growonder*

• **Don't have a backyard?** You don't need one to have a garden. Get help at "Garden in Unbelievable Places": *urbanext.uiuc.edu/firstgarden/planning/unusual_00.html*

• **Fun activities with Defenders of Wildlife:** *www.kidsplanet.org/defendit/new/enjoyit.html*

*There's a lot more to see and do at **50simplekids.com***

21. DON'T GET BUGGED!

Take a Guess:
Which are there more of on the Earth?
A) People B) Ants C) Dogs

Bugs! Ugh! What good are they?
You'd be surprised!
Bugs are an important part of keeping the Earth healthy. In fact we couldn't live without them!

Really? Really!

Did You Know

• Worms may be gross, but believe it or not, we wouldn't be able to grow food without them. Why? Because they eat their way through dirt and leave behind rich soil that plants love.

• In an area about the size of a football field, you could find close to two million worms!

• Bees are necessary, too. As they travel from flower to flower gathering pollen to make honey (they travel 55,000 miles and pollinate two million flowers just to make one pound of honey!), they spread pollen to other plants as well. The plants can then make seeds, which means more of them will grow. Because we need plants to stay alive, we owe the bees a lot!

• There are more than 2,000 different kinds of spiders in

Answer: B. There are more ants than people or dogs, even more than both added together!

America. Sure they're scary, but they really make our lives better. Why? Because they eat other bugs like mosquitoes and flies. Without spiders we'd be overrun with bugs. In fact scientists guess that the bugs spiders eat in one year weigh as much as all the people on the Earth! That's heavy!

What You Can Do

• Next time you see a bug on the sidewalk, help it out. Gently pick it up and move it out of the way, where no one will step on it. You've just saved a life!

• Adopt a spider. Watch it. Admire it. Get grossed out by it. But don't kill it. When you see a spider spin its web, catch a fly and even—ugh!—eat it, you're watching a real-life adventure that's even better than TV!

• Always look in the tub before you turn the water on. Spiders love to hang out there.

• If you find a bug in your house, help it to get outside—or leave it alone and let it find its own way out. The bug probably never meant to visit you, and wandered into your house by accident. Note: If it's a stinging bug, ask for an adult's help in moving it.

Amaze Your Friends

Give them this "Amazing Bug" quiz:

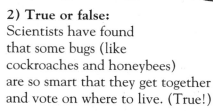

1) True or false: Bees use a special dance to tell other bees where to find flowers. (True! It's called *waggle* dancing.)

2) True or false: Scientists have found that some bugs (like cockroaches and honeybees) are so smart that they get together and vote on where to live. (True!)

3) True or false: Beetles are popular pets in Japan. (True! You can buy them in department stores.)

4) True or false: We have to be especially careful with honeybees, because they're starting to disappear. (Unfortunately, true. And no one knows exactly why.)

See for Yourself

• **Join the Bug Club!** If you have a real passion for bugs, you can join the bug club: *amentsoc.org/bug-club/*

• **Watch "The Bug Hunt":**
youtube.com/watch?v=OlFlNtux4nk&feature=user

• **Play The Great Bug Hunt:** *ecokids.ca/pub/games_ activities/wildlife/index.cfm*

• **Bug facts:** *parents-choice.org/article.cfm?art_id=147& the_page=consider_this*

• **Hunt for bugs in the garden!** Use a magnifying glass to look for bugs in the "garden"…then get info about them: *fossweb.com/modulesK-2/Insects/activities/insecthunt.html*

22. IT'S THE LAW!

Take a Guess:
How do we know when a species is endangered?
A) It hides in the basement B) It sends you an e-mail
C) Scientists tell us there aren't many left

Extinction is a word you might have heard.
When people say an animal or plant is *extinct*, that means it doesn't exist anymore; you can't find it anywhere on the Earth.

Dinosaurs are the most famous extinct species. They died out long ago…but other animals and plants are becoming extinct *right now!*

In fact, *every single week* many species of plants and animals disappear somewhere in the world. Poof!…They're gone. Just like that.

And many more species are *endangered*—which means they're getting *close* to extinction. That includes animals like tigers, elephants, and pandas.

Shouldn't we be doing something about this?

Well, some of us are trying. We have a law to protect these species. It's called the *Endangered Species Act.* You can help people learn how important it is!

Answer: C. It is science that determines whether a species is "endangered."

Did You Know

- The Endangered Species Act became a law in 1973. It was the *first law in history* to say that people in a country should protect *all* the species that live there.

- It has already protected hundreds of species from extinction, including the bald eagle, the grizzly bear, the Pacific salmon, and the gray whale.

- Protecting one species from extinction helps many other species, too. Different species depend on each other for food, shelter, and other support. So, if one species dies out, many others will, too.

- The Endangered Species Act doesn't just protect species —it also protects the places they live, called *habitats*. This is very important, because one of the main reasons animals become extinct is habitat destruction.

What You Can Do

- Take the Kids Endangered Species Pledge—and tell your friends about it, too: *www.nwf.org/endangered/kidspledge.cfm*

- Find out about an endangered species living in your area at: *www.enature.com/zipguides/index.asp?choice=endangered* Draw a picture of it and send it to your congressperson. Find their name and contact here: *capwiz.com/wcs/dbq/officials/* (You might need a grown-up to help you with this.)

At School

Celebrate *Endangered Species Day* on the third Friday in May. The official web site has lots of ideas for you and your teacher: *stopextinction.org/cgi-bin/giga.cgi?cmd=cause_dir_custom&cause_id=1704&page=daykit*

Amaze Your Friends

Tell your teacher and classmates about the incredible Tour de Turtles. Some folks who are working to save endangered sea turtles came up with a way for us to watch them and see how they do it.

They followed the journey of eight sea turtles across the ocean. You can follow along at: *tourdeturtles.megotta.com/Home.aspx* (For teachers: *tourdeturtles.org/activities.html*)

See for Yourself

• **The Antiguan Racer Conservation Project.** An amazing true story: *www.antiguanracer.org/html/home.htm*

• **Arkive.** Lots of information, videos, and photos of endangered species: *www.arkive.org/threatened-species/*

• **Defenders of Wildlife.** Learn about endangered species: *kidsplanet.org/factsheets/map.html* and *kidsplanet.org/cyw/*

• **American Museum of Natural History.** Click on *amnh.org/ology/index.php?channel=biodiversity*

23. SAVE THE WHALES

Take a Guess:
Which of these is really a whale?
A) A ballet dancer   B) A dolphin   C) A football player

Whales are the largest animals that have ever lived on Earth—even larger than dinosaurs!

Unfortunately, some whales are starting to follow in the dinosaurs' footsteps…even though whales don't even have feet. They're in danger of becoming extinct—and *that's* not a joke.

These magnificent creatures are threatened by whaling, garbage, chemicals, noise, fishing lines, and more. But you can do a little something to help protect them.

Did You Know

• Whales are *mammals*, which means they're warm-blooded and breathe air—like us—although they live in the water.

• A whale's nose is on top of its head and is called a *blowhole*. A single breath from a blue whale can inflate 2,000 balloons!

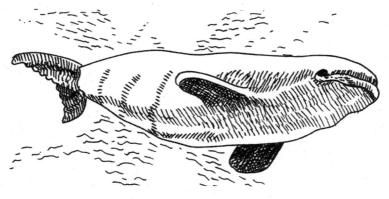

Answer: B. Technically, a dolphin is a type of whale! Did you know that?

- The largest whales are blue whales…in fact, they are the largest creatures *ever* to live on Earth.

- Ten whale species are on the endangered list, including the *baleen*, *blue*, and *right* whales.

What You Can Do

- Become a Greenpeace Whale Defender. Greenpeace has been saving whales for over 30 years. They can show you how to write letters to newspapers and political leaders, and how to help get people to pay attention to whales' problems: *greenpeace.org/usa/campaigns/oceans/whale-defenders/iwc/kids-get-involved*

- Many organizations work to save whales. Your family or school can help them by "adopting" a whale. You can find them here: *whalevideo.com/*

At School

- Have a whale fundraiser, like the first-grade class at Glenbrook Elementary School in Calgary, Alberta, Canada. They had a "Bake Sale to Save a Whale" and lemonade stand—plus they made and sold "whale whistles." They raised over $400 and used the money for Adopt-a-Whale kits.

- For ideas, download Greenpeace's "Bake Sale for the Whales" kit: *members.greenpeace.org/event/launch/138/*

Amaze your friends

See Whales in Action!

• If you live near an ocean or aquarium, you might be able to see live whales. Check these sites: *anctuarycruises. com* or *neaq.org/visit_planning/whale_watch/index.php*

• If not, movies about whales are great. For example: Subscribe to Dan the Whaleman's videos on YouTube: *youtube.com/user/danthewhaleman* or get his DVDs, "Awesome Whales For Kids" and "Salt & Friends: Humpback Whales With Names" at *whalevideo.com/titles.htm*

See for Yourself

• **Learn all about whales** and other marine mammals: *www.afsc.noaa.gov/nmml/education/*
This is a great site to show your teachers and parents, too.

• **The Whales: Voices in the Sea,** is an online exhibit— whale calls, games, videos: *cetus.ucsd.edu/voicesinthesea_org/Flash/*

• **Play the Humpback Whale Migration Game:** *sanctuaries.noaa.gov/whales/main_ page.html.*

There's a lot more to see and do at **50simplekids.com**

24. SUPPORT A ZOO OR AQUARIUM

Take a Guess:
Why do zoos help endangered animals to have families?
A) They like diapers   B) They want to protect wildlife
C) None of your business

Elephants, camels, giraffes, penguins, snakes, flamingos, alligators, sharks…and people—all in the same place. Only at zoos and aquariums!

Zoos and aquariums have always been places people could go to see different kinds of animals. But today, these places are doing something else that is important, too. They are working to help keep endangered animals alive. We need to support them!

Did You Know

• The Philadelphia Zoo, America's first zoo, opened in 1874—more than 125 years ago! The first public aquarium was even earlier. It opened in 1856, in New York City.

Answer: B. And endangered species need all the help they can get!

• At first, zoos just put animals in cages for people to look at. But over the years, zoos and aquariums have become more involved with education and with *conservation*—which means they are trying to save the animals from extinction.

• Some zoos have created areas that look and feel like the animals' real homes. At the San Diego Zoo, for example, tigers and Malayan sun bears live in special places that look just like the Asian rainforests they come from.

• In these more-natural zoo areas, many rare types of animals, like jaguars, are even able to have babies.

• That's very good news. But building special areas and raising babies takes a lot of money!

What You Can Do

• Support your local zoo or aquarium by visiting it whenever you can. You can even volunteer to help out!

• Consider having your next birthday party at the zoo. It's a way to help support it, learn a lot, and have tons of fun at the same time!

• If there's no zoo or aquarium near you, you can visit one online. There are hundreds of fun zoo web sites! Many have online programs and camps for kids! For example check out the National Zoo's site: *nationalzoo.si.edu/Education/CampsClasses/*

• Most zoos have "adopt an animal" programs. Money from this goes into keeping the zoo running properly. It's not cheap—"adoptions" normally start at $25—but it's something you can share with a bunch of friends or your whole class at school.

Amaze Your Friends

We think these web sites are amazing—if your friends like zoos, they will, too. These sites will get you to…

—40 international zoo sites: *greatbluemarble.com/Zoos.htm*

—More than 100 U.S. zoo sites: *exzooberance.com/zoo%20 and%20aquarium%20directory.htm*

See for Yourself

• **Design a panda habitat:** *nationalzoo.si.edu/education/ conservationcentral/design/default.cfm*

• **Games about endangered species,** from the San Diego Zoo: *sandiegozoo.org/kids/games/index.html*

• **Zoo history:** *www.kidcyber.com.au/topics/zoos.htm*

• **An animal survival game!** *zoovetgame.com/*

There's a lot more to see and do at **50simplekids.com**

25. EVERY LITTER BIT HURTS

Take a Guess:
Which of these is considered litter?
A) A goose   B) A banana tree   C) A candy wrapper

Riddle: When is a street like a garbage can?
Answer: When there's litter in it!

That's not very funny, is it? Candy wrappers, soda cans, old newspapers, and other garbage on the ground make it look as though no one cares about the Earth.

But that's not the worst thing about litter. It can also be harmful to animals. It can even kill them.

So, every time you get ready to toss out your trash, you have a chance to protect some special creatures.

Did You Know

• Cigarette butts, snack wrappers, take-out boxes, and drink containers are our most common litter. Each one can hurt animals in a different way.

• Little animals like squirrels and skunks sometimes stick their heads in small plastic containers (especially

Answer: C. Almost anything you throw on the ground and leave there is litter!

yogurt containers) trying to get the food that's left, and get stuck there. They die because they can't eat.

• Deer and other animals often cut their tongues on half-opened cans.

• Six-pack rings can trap and strangle birds, fish, and other animals.

• We toss out billions of cigarette butts, which are made of plastic, every year. Animals mistake them for food and eat them—which can kill them.

What You Can Do

• Throw garbage in trash cans, not on the ground.

• If you see trash lying on the ground, take time to put it in the garbage.

• When you go for a hike with your friends or family, bring some bags along for trash—the trash you make along the way as well as trash you find.

• Snip your six-pack rings—cut the rings so no animal can get stuck in them.

At School

• Organize a "Litter Drive" like they did at Middleton Elementary School in Sherwood, Oregon.

- Two fifth-graders worked with their teacher and principal to create a plan to reduce litter at school.

- Their class bought trash cans and put on an assembly about litter. Then they organized a schoolwide cleanup day. You can do it, too!

Amaze Your Friends

How long does litter last? Probably a lot longer than they think. So ask them: If you throw something on the ground, how long before it becomes part of the Earth again?

1) A piece of paper? (**Answer:** *A month*), **2)** A woolen sock? (*A year*), **3)** Aluminum soda can? (*At least 200 years*), **4)** Banana peel? (*3–5 weeks*), **5)** A disposable diaper? (*20–30 years*), **6)** Plastic six-pack rings? (*450 years*), **7)** Glass bottle? (*A really, really, really long time. Maybe a million years*), **8)** Batteries? (*100 years*), **9)** Plastic bags? (*10–20 years*), **10)** Plastic soda bottle? (*It lasts so long, we might just as well say "forever."*)

See for Yourself

- **Check out this photo!** It's a skunk with its head stuck in a yogurt container. Read the story, too! *www.flickr.com/photos/marilynphotos/2636801620/*

- **Litter hurts animals!** Read more about it on this site: *pleasebekind.com/dontlitter.html*

- **Two sites about litter in the ocean:**

    —*marine-litter.gpa.unep.org/kids/kids.htm*

    —*marinedebris.noaa.gov/marinedebris101/ActivBk_pop.html*

- **Litter animation:** *youtube.com/watch?v=SVZfjvA2k3k*

26. HOME, TWEET HOME

Take a Guess:
Where do birds live?
A) In nests made of twigs B) In undergound burrows
C) In milk cartons

Everyone knows that birds build their own nests. So, why should you build a house for a bird? Or a home for a bat, a toad or a squirrel?

It's sad to say, but animals all over the world are losing their homes...and when they have no place to live, they can die out.

You can help an animal family find a place to stay. And you don't need anything fancy—just an old milk carton or ceramic bowl.

Did You Know

You can build a birdhouse out of a milk carton.

You'll need:

- One empty half-gallon cardboard milk carton
- A pair of scissors
- About two feet of wire—light enough to bend, strong enough to hold the weight of the birdhouse
- Two nails and a hammer
- Dried grass or dog hair
- Some packing tape (waterproof)

Answer: In all of them.

Instructions

1) First, completely open up the top of the carton and wash it thouroughly with soap.

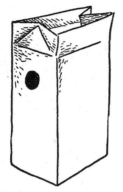

2) Take the scissors and cut a hole about the size of a doorknob in one side of the milk carton, a few inches below the top folds. This is the "door."

3) On the other side of the carton, make two holes—one above the other—with a nail. The top hole should be about 1/3 of the way down from the top. The bottom hole should be 1/3 of the way up from the bottom.

4) Now put the wire through the top nail hole, along the inside of the carton, and out the bottom hole.

5) Make a bed for the birds by putting some of the dried grass or dog hair on the carton bottom.

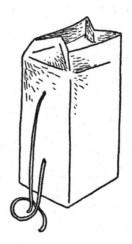

6) Close the top of the carton. Seal it tight with the tape.

7) Find a pole or tree outside that's not surrounded by other trees, poles, or buildings. (Keep it close to home so you can enjoy it!) Bang the nails in with the hammer, about a foot apart, one above the other.

8) Hang the birdhouse on the nails by wrapping one end of the wire around one nail, and the other end around the other nail. Make sure it's good and tight, so the carton will stay up. You're done!

See for Yourself

• **Toad-ally cool!** Toads are bumpy, slimy creatures that help gardens *and* the Earth. They need special damp, dark places to live. You can build a toad house with a flower pot, a pie pan, and some paint. Go to: *projectwildlife.org/gardens_toadhouse.htm*

Also: *familycrafts.about.com/od/frogcrafts/ig/toadville*

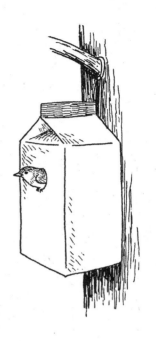

• **Build a bat house.** Good step-by-step instructions: *thisoldhouse.com/toh/how-to/intro/0,,20165965,00.html* (parents need to help with this). And here's a good video: *thisoldhouse.com/toh/video/0,,20166044,00.html*

• **Build a squirrel house.** Get links to kids' stories about squirrels, a squirrel-house journal, a squirrel quiz, and more: *tricklecreekbooks.com/squirrelhousecontents.htm* Then find out how to build a squirrel house: *tricklecreekbooks.com/squirrelsneedhomestoo.htm*

• **More birdhouses:**

—*thekidsgarden.co.uk/BuildA-BirdHouse.html*

—*helium.com/knowledge/65407how-to-make-a-simple-birdhouse-out-of-craft-sticks*

—Links for owl houses: *owlpages.com/links.php?cat=Owls-Nest+Boxes*

27. OH, GIVE THEM A HOME...

Take a Guess:
Where do the deer and the antelope stay?
A) In apartment houses B) At hotels   C) Home, home on the range

Where do you live? In a house?...An apartment?... On a farm or a ranch? Does it get really cold and snowy in the place you call home...or do you live where it's always nice and hot?

There are many different kinds of places for people to live. Wild animals need different kinds of places to live, too. So do plants, trees, and grasses. Their homes are called *habitats*.

Unfortunately, in order to make more places for *people* to live, we have destroyed a lot of the habitat that other living things need.

As the forests, fields, and swamps they call home disappear, so do the animals and plants. They can't survive without their homes.

That's why the U.S. government has set aside large areas of water and land where habitat is protected forever. This

Answer: C, of course. "And the skies are not cloudy all day."

land is called the National Wildlife Refuge System. It needs your support!

Did You Know

• There are over 540 National Wildlife Refuges in the United States—at least one in every state.

• The refuges provide homes for 700 bird species, 220 mammal species, 250 reptile and amphibian species, and more than 200 kinds of fish.

• Almost 40 million people visit refuges every year. There's a refuge within an hour's drive of every major city in the United States. And many specialize in school groups and tours! Is there one near you?

What You Can Do

• Buy a federal Junior Duck Stamp for $5. The money raised goes directly to wildlife refuges: *calwaterfowl.org/duck_stamp/index.htm*

• Visit a wildlife refuge with your family or class. Use this map to find the closest one: *www.fws.gov/refuges/refuge LocatorMaps/index.html* (or call 1-800-344-WILD)

• Join a Friends of the Refuge group with your family: *www.refugenet.org/new-friends-connect/index-frgp.html*

• Celebrate National Wildlife Refuge Week in October: *defenders.org/take_action/upcoming_events/national_wildlife_ refuge_week.php*

Amaze Your Friends

It's hard work to protect animals' habitats. Prove it to your friends. Challenge them to design a habitat for the black-footed ferret in this game: *arkiveeducation.org/ games_habitat.html*

See for Yourself

- **Learn about the web of life**—all about species and habitat—from a friendly garden spider: *kidsplanet.org/wol/*

- **"Creature Features" from National Geographic Kids:** *kids.nationalgeographic.com/Animals/CreatureFeature/*

- **Online park fun with the National Park Service:** *nps.gov/learn/parkfun.htm*

- **Games** about animals and their habitats: *arkiveeducation.org/games.html*

- **Check these out!** Photos and facts about habitat for you and your parents from National Geographic: *environment.nationalgeographic.com/environment/habitats/*

There's a lot more to see and do at **50simplethings.com**

KEEPING
THE

EARTH
GREEN

THINKING GREEN

If you look green, you're probably not feeling very well. But if the Earth is green, it's a healthy planet.

A green Earth means that plants are growing. It means that the soil is good, there's plenty of water, the air is clean, animals have places to live and things to eat.

And some wonderful news: Anyone can help keep the Earth green. It's so easy. You can plant a seed, give it some water and watch it grow. You can save paper so that fewer trees will be cut down. You can "adopt" plants that are already growing and help them enjoy life.

Another important thing about plants (especially trees): they help fight global warming and give us oxygen, which is the air we need to live.

What a deal!

We need lots of greenery in our world. Let's start planting!

28. DON'T BAG IT!

Take a Guess:
What's the best type of bag to use when you go shopping?
A) Plastic   B) Cloth   C) Paper

Did you ever stop to think how weird it is that everything we buy gets put in bags?...Even when it's only one item, like a candy bar...or a bag of chips? A bag in a bag—now that's crazy!

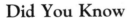

But it happens all the time. And then we just throw the bag away.

What a waste! Bags are made from the Earth's treasures. Paper bags are made out of trees; plastic bags are made from oil. And manufacturing both of them adds a lot of pollution. But you can help. Just say "No" to bags you don't really need.

Did You Know

• Americans use 40 billion grocery bags in a year. How many is that? Think of it this way: It would take you over 1,200 years just to *count* them all! And that's just the *grocery* bags.

• Another way to look at it: Count to five. "1-2-3-4-5"...and guess what—we just used another 60,000 bags in the U.S.!

• Today alone, Americans used over 100 million grocery bags. And we do the same thing every day.

Answer: B. Cloth is best—you can use it over and over again.

What You Can Do

• Next time you buy something small, tell the clerk you don't need a bag for it. Just say politely, "No thanks, I'm protecting the planet."

• If you don't notice the clerk putting your things into a bag don't be afraid to give it back. Say, "Sorry, I really don't need this." Even if the clerk looks at you funny, you'll feel great knowing you're doing the right thing.

• Buy some cloth bags and bring them with you whenever you shop. There are lots of places to find cheap ones. Some grocery stores sell them for as little as $1.

Reuse Bags!

• If you do take a paper or plastic shopping bag, try to reuse it.

• When you go shopping, bring paper or plastic bags saved from another shopping trip.

• An average U.S. family could save 55 pounds of paper a year just by reusing paper grocery bags three times before recycling!

• Sometimes even your parents need reminding. So, help them remember to put paper, plastic, or cloth bags in the car for future shopping.

Amaze Your Friends

Take them on a bag-counting field trip at the supermarket.

Watch people leaving the store for 10 or 15 minutes. Try counting all the bags they've got. Then imagine people all over the U.S. leaving supermarkets every day with all those bags. Imagine how many trees are being cut down and how much plastic is used in a single day just for carrying groceries. Wow!

See for Yourself

• **Make your own cloth shopping bags!** This site has patterns for 35 different bags—including ones made from old pillowcases and old jeans. (You might need some help from parents on this.) *tipnut.com/35-reusable-grocery-bags-totes-free-patterns*

• **Can't find cloth bags you like?** Check out these cool ones, including one made out of recycled juice boxes! *reusablebags.com/store/shopping-bags-kids-bags-c-2_45.html*

• **How to recycle plastic bags.** Detailed instructions: *ehow.com/how_10885_recycle-plastic-grocery.html*

• **If kids ruled the world.** A video starring little kids: *youtube.com/watch?v=4ZntqsuSdvY*

*There's a lot more to see and do at **50simplekids.com***

29. PLANT A TREE

Take a Guess:
What does an apple tree produce besides apples?
A) Air to help us breathe   B) TV shows   C) Lemons

Can you think of anything that gives us paper, fruit, nuts, lumber, places for birds and animals to live and places for kids to climb, and *also* helps keep our air clean (now here's the tricky part) *besides* trees?

Think hard; take your time. If you can come up with the right answer, you can help save the Earth.

Are you ready?

The answer is…No. Nothing can take the place of trees—that's why they're so important.

We need to keep the world full of trees. You can help make this happen. You can plant one.

Did You Know

• According to some experts, the average American uses seven trees a year in paper, wood, and other products made from trees. That's over 1-1/2 billion trees a year!

• Trees help fight global warming by absorbing *carbon dioxide*, a gas that animals and people produce when they exhale. Carbon dioxide is also produced by cars and factories, which burn oil and coal.

• Once there wasn't so much carbon

Answer: A. All trees (and plants) produce oxygen…and help keep us breathing.

dioxide in the air, but today there is too much. Why? There are millions of cars and factories all over the world putting carbon dioxide into the air at the same time, and billions of trees that could have absorbed it have been cut down—so there aren't enough trees left to do the work.

• Trees also provide shade. In hot weather, a house with a few good shade trees next to it is a lot cooler than one without shade trees. That house will need much less energy for air-conditioning—10%–50% less!—and that means less coal burned to make energy, which is definitely an Earth-saver!

• Planting a tree is great fun, and one of the best things you can do to save the Earth. The tree will reduce the carbon dioxide in the air, provide beauty and shade, and attract wildlife. Every year, you and your tree will grow, proud to know you're both helping the Earth.

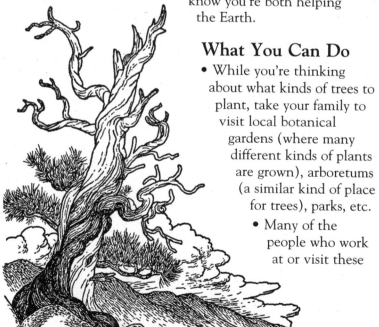

What You Can Do

• While you're thinking about what kinds of trees to plant, take your family to visit local botanical gardens (where many different kinds of plants are grown), arboretums (a similar kind of place for trees), parks, etc.

• Many of the people who work at or visit these

places are very knowledgeable and helpful, and can help you answer questions, such as: What kinds of trees grow fast and need little extra water? What kinds attract birds and animals? Talk about this with those tree lovers and your family.

• Go to a local nursery or gardening center with your mom or dad. Talk with the people who work there to figure out what kind of tree to plant…and where. How much space do you have? What kind of soil? What's the weather like?

• Be sure to choose a spot that has the right amount of sunlight and good soil drainage—too much drainage means the dirt will be too dry; too little means it'll stay too damp and the tree's roots could rot.

• We don't have enough space here to tell you all the steps to planting a tree. But we do have room to tell you that planting a tree is a lot easier than you might think. For more tips and very helpful tree planting information, check out the sites under See for Yourself.

• Think about talking with neighbors, friends, and people at school to see if you can start a community tree-planting effort. You'll be surprised by how many people will love the idea—especially after you explain how important trees are and what a good way to save the Earth this is.

See for Yourself

• **Carly's Kids' Corner** at the Arbor Day Foundation. Lots of games and activities: *arborday.org/kids/carly/*

• **Tree Musketeers,** a group created for kids by kids: *treemusketeers.org/tm06/index.asp*

• **The Secret Life of Trees:** *urbanext.uiuc.edu/trees2/*

• **Trees Are Terrific!** Interactive fun: *urbanext.uiuc.edu/trees1/flash/index.html*

• **Take a Walk in the Woods:** *urbanext.uiuc.edu/woods/*

• **Learn about Trees with Dr. Arbor:** *urbanext.uiuc.edu/trees3/01.html*

• **For parents and teachers.** Info and experiments about trees and leaves: *kidsgardening.com/Dig/DigDetail. taf?ID=1334&Type=Art*

There's a lot more to see and do at **50simplekids.com**

30. GET GROWING

Take a Guess:
Which of these is easiest to grow indoors on your windowsill?
A) A cabbage patch   B) An avocado plant   C) A lightbulb

Riddle: What is more complicated than a computer, "runs" on water and light instead of batteries or electricity, and even comes in chocolate and vanilla? Here's a big hint—it's green.

Answer: A plant. (Remember, cocoa beans and vanilla beans come from plants.)

When you think about it, plants are pretty amazing. Every plant, no matter how big or small, helps make our air cleaner and our Earth greener.

Our Earth needs all the help it can get. And you can do something just by planting a seed and adding water! As you take care of it and watch it grow, you can feel good knowing that you're also helping to take care of our Earth.

Did You Know

• All plants and animals need each other. Plants make the oxygen that people and animals breathe; people and animals exhale the carbon dioxide that plants need to live.

• Plants help reduce air pollution by absorbing some pollutants from the air.

• Every day bulldozers tear up many plants to make room for more streets, parking lots, homes, and businesses.

Answer: B. You need an avocado pit, a couple of toothpicks, and a glass of water.

• If every person in the United States planted a couple of seeds, there would soon be over 300 million more plants growing and making the Earth a healthier place to live.

What You Can Do

Grow Some Greenery at Home!

• Decide what you'd like to grow. Salad greens, flowers, and herbs are easy to grow in containers on a sunny windowsill.

• There are lots of different kinds of salad greens to choose from, such as red-leaf lettuce or butter lettuce. The first time you help prepare a salad made with lettuce grown in your very own garden, you'll be so proud! And you'll be amazed at how good and fresh it will taste.

• Lots of herbs used to flavor our foods are easy to grow from seeds—like chives, parsley, oregano, dill, and others. Certain flowers are easy, too, like alyssum, petunias, and marigolds.

• You can buy the seeds you want at a plant nursery, online, or even at many hardware stores. While you're there, also buy some potting soil and a little plant food (organic, please!) such as liquid fish emulsion.

• Get all the details you need to grow plants at home or at school from the web sites included at the end of this chapter, under See for Yourself.

Grow Some Greenery at School!

• Kids at Washburn Elementary School in Washburn, Wisconsin, and the San Jose, California, Montessori School plant their own school gardens and then eat many school lunches using food they've planted themselves!

• Hinkle Elementary's fourth-grade class created this web site all about plants: *library.thinkquest.org/3715/*

Amaze Your Friends

Ask them if these "growing" statements are true or false

1) There are *2 billion* bacteria in just one teaspoon of soil … plus millions more fungi, protozoa, and algae! *True.*

2) Scientists believe they've identified a flower that is 120 million years old.

3) There are over 500 types of meat-eating plants growing in the world. (And some will even eat beef!) *True.*

4) Bamboo can grow three feet in just one day. *True again!*

Yes, they're all true—it's an amazing world!

See for Yourself

• **Fun with plants!** Help Detective LePlant and his partners, Bud and Sprout, unlock the amazing mysteries of plant life! *www.urbanext.uiuc.edu/gpe/index.html*

• **Your first garden!** *urbanext.uiuc.edu/firstgarden/*

• **Plants for all ages!** The nice part about this site is that on the left side of the screen you can pick your age: *bbc.co.uk/schools/scienceclips/ages/5_6/growing_plants.shtml*

• **Watch this!** Plants grow right before your very eyes! *plantsinmotion.bio.indiana.edu/plantmotion/starthere.html*

• **Get small!** Go on a dirt safari and micro-size yourself to look at what is really going on in the dirt: *school.discoveryeducation.com/schooladventures/soil/*

• **Read this!** To find out more about growing plants both indoors and out, check out the book *Kids Gardening: A Kid's Guide to Messing Around in the Dirt*, by Kim and Kevin Raftery.

There's a lot more to see and do at **50simplekids.com**

31. BE A
PAPER SAVER

Take a Guess:

*If you stacked up all the paper an average American
uses in a year, the pile would be as tall as...*
A) A car   B) A pickle   C) A two-story house

It takes a year for a tree to grow enough to be made into paper. And it takes many forests to make all the paper we use...and throw away.

Wouldn't it be great if old paper could be turned back into new paper? Then we'd have more trees and a greener world.

We can make that happen—there is a way. We can recycle our paper.

Does that really work? You bet! Want proof? Take a good look at this book—it's printed on recycled paper!

Did You Know

• Americans use 90 million tons of paper every year, about 600 pounds for each person.

• How much is that? The paper a four-person family uses in just one year weighs as much as a big car!

• To make all that paper, we use more than a billion trees!

Answer: C. Believe it or not, as high as a two-story house.

• If everyone in the U.S. recycled their newspapers (including the comics), we'd save 500,000 trees every week.

• How is paper recycled? It's shredded and mashed into a glob called *pulp*, which is then turned back into paper. It's so simple you can do it yourself! (See the Eco-experiments at the end of the book.)

What You Can Do
At Home

• Recycle all kinds of paper—cereal boxes, note paper, bags, newspaper, etc.

• To start recycling, first find a place where you can put a pile of newspapers and a box or two for collecting other types of paper.

• Whenever you empty a cereal box, or finish using a piece of paper, put it in the recycling box instead of the garbage. If you get a newspaper, stack it on the pile every day.

• If you've tried Simple Thing #7 (*Be a Recycling Detective*), then you already know what paper can be recycled in your area, how to prepare it, and where to recycle it. If you haven't done #7 yet, go back and give it a shot.

At School

Many schoolkids in Pasco County, Florida, are part of the "Earth Patrol." They are responsible for collecting the recyclable paper and making sure it ends up in the proper bins. Their school district has been nationally recognized for its achievements: *paperrecycles.org/recycling_awards/pasco_county.html*

Amaze Your Friends

Get them to collect all the recyclable paper in their houses for one week. Then weigh it on a scale at home to see how much paper their family uses in one week. Multiply this by 52 (the number of weeks in a year) to find out how many pounds of paper their family uses each year. You might be amazed!

See for Yourself

• **How recycled paper is made:** *paperrecycles.org/school_recycling/curb_to_consumer/index.html*

• **Buster's paper quiz:** *ollierecycles.com/uk/html/paper_spot.html*

• **Watch this!** A video about making recycled paper: *metacafe.com/watch/1063787/how_to_recycle_paper/*

There's a lot more to see and do at **50simplekids.com**

32. HELP PROTECT THE RAINFOREST

Take a Guess:

How much of the Earth's rainforest is destroyed every minute?
A) Enough to fill a parking lot   B) Enough to fill a movie theater
C) Enough to fill 60 football fields

D oesn't the word "rainforest" sound exotic and far away? What does it have to do with you? Why is everyone talking about rainforests now, anyway? What's so important about them?

Tropical rainforests are thick, wet forests that are the homes of amazing people and wonderful animals—like parrots, monkeys, and jaguars.

There are so many trees in our rainforests that they actually affect the weather all around the world. They even affect the air we breathe.

In recent years, people have been cutting down the rainforests. This must be stopped, and you can help.

Did You Know

• Although rainforests cover only a small part of the Earth, they're home to over half the world's plants and animals. Many are losing their homes as the forests are cut down.

Answer: C. Incredible, but true!

- Rainforest plants give us some of our most important medicines for cancer, heart disease, and other illnesses. As rainforests get torn down, we can lose many of these plants—and the cures they could help produce—forever.

- It's estimated that rainforests are being cut down at the rate of about 100 acres per *minute*—fast enough to cut down all our rainforests in a few decades.

What You Can Do

At Home

- Learn— and teach!— about the fascinating and wonderful plants, animals, and people of the world's rainforests.

- Don't buy hamburgers at fast-food restaurants that use beef from cattle raised on land that was once a rainforest.

- Ask your parents not to buy products made out of tropical rainforest wood—rosewood, mahogany, teak, and ebony. Learn more from the Rainforest Action Network: *ran.org/ new/kidscorner/about_rainforests/factsheets/facts_about_wood/*

At School

- Write or e-mail your U.S. senators and ask them to help protect the rainforests. Address your letters to: (The name of your Senator), U.S. Senate, Washington, D.C. 20515

There are lots of ways to raise money to help protect rainforests. For example:

• **A performance:** Patrick Henry Elementary School in Long Beach, California, put on a play and asked for donations for the rainforest. With the money they collected, they bought a piece of the rainforest.

• **A "penny harvest":** First graders at Remsen Elementary in New York raised $17.50 by collecting pennies and donated the money to help the rainforest.

• What will your class do?

Amaze Your Friends

• Show them what just one kid can accomplish! Check out *kidssavingtherainforest.org* and read about a group started by two girls to help save the rainforest in Costa Rica. Now they've accomplished *incredible* things: building monkey bridges, an animal shelter, a reforestation program, a kids' camp, and a whole lot more!

See for Yourself

There are lots of great kids' sites about the rainforest. Here are four:

• *rainforest-alliance.org/programs/ education/kids*

• *ran.org/new/kidscorner*

• *news.mongabay.com/*

• *nature.org/rainforests/ explore/quiz.html*

There's a lot more to see and do at **50simplekids.com**

33. EAT YOUR NEIGHBOR'S FOOD!

Take a Guess:
What can you find on a farm?
A) Fresh fruit   B) Giant robots   C) An orchestra

W hat? Are we telling you to sneak into your neighbors' home, and take the food right off their plates? Of course not!

The neighbors we're talking about are the farmers who live near you. They grow delicious, nutritious food...and they *want* you to eat it.

Take a look at the labels on the food in your kitchen. See where it comes from. You'll find that some of it was grown or made in faraway places. That means a lot of energy was used—and pollution was created—just to get it to you. But why buy food from halfway around the world when you can get it from producers who live nearby?

Eating local food means you can save some of the Earth's treasures...plus, it means your food will be fresher and better-tasting. What a deal!

Did You Know

• If you're an average American, each of your meals has ingredients from at least five countries outside the U.S.

Answer: A. Farms grow all kinds of delicious fruit!

- For example, over 250 million pounds of grapes are sent from Chile to Los Angeles, California, every year. These grapes travel 5,900 miles in cargo ships and trucks, which creates 7,000 tons of global warming pollution—the same amount created by over 1,200 cars.

- Even food grown in the U.S. is often trucked long distances from huge farms. A head of romaine lettuce typically travels 2,055 miles from farm to store; a stalk of celery averages 1,788 miles; an onion, 1,675 miles. Check out a map and see how far that is!

- Here's another thing to think about: Buying food that is grown nearby supports local farmers and protects their farmland. If they can sell their food, then they won't have to sell their farms to people who will build houses on them.

What You Can Do

- Find out what foods are grown in your area during the year: *www.epicurious.com/articlesguides/ seasonalcooking/farmtotable/ seasonalingredientmap* or *nrdc.org/health/foodmiles/*

- Make it a project: You and your family can agree to spend $10 a week on local food, or just decide to eat one locally produced food each week: *foodroutes.org/buy-local-challenge.jsp*

- Take the Eat Local Challenge in October with your family or class, and eat only local foods for a whole week: *eatlocal.net* (or try this any time of year).

- Talk to the folks at your favorite restaurant about using local foods.

Amaze Your Friends

Take them on a treasure hunt to find local foods. Get a grown-up to help you find:

- **A farmers' market** (where farmers come to your town and set up a stand)

- **A U-pick or farm stand** (where you go to the farm and pick the food yourself)

- **A food co-op** (a kind of grocery store that sells lots of local foods)

- **A CSA** (*community-supported agriculture*): This is a farm that people pay to join. Every week or two, members get a box of fresh vegetables grown on the farm.

See for Yourself

- **Use these web sites** to find farms and stores where you live: *localharvest.org* (local farms), *eatwellguide.org* or *organic.org/storefinder* or *pickyourown.org* (U-pick farms)

- **Watch this!** A funny video about buying local: *youtube.com/watch?v=NPct1usF8oA*

- **And this!** A video about a CSA: *youtube.com/watch?v=DUBf_a3EtQU&NR=1*

- **Spatulatta**—a kid's cooking web site, hosted by two sisters who are kids themselves: *spatulatta.com*

- **A–Z** slide show: *cuesa.org/sustainable_ag/A-Z/*

34. GOOD FOR YOU, GOOD FOR THE EARTH

Take a Guess:
When food is "organic," it means:
A) It knows how to play the organ   B) It's very organized
C) It's grown without pesticides or other harmful chemicals

Everyone will tell you that eating fresh fruits and vegetables is good for you. And they're right! Here's another good thing to know: The best fruits and veggies are ones that are good for the *Earth*, too! That's what *organic food* is: food that's grown in harmony with nature, that's healthy for people *and* wildlife, and that doesn't pollute our air, water, or soil.

Did You Know

• Organic food is grown without harmful chemicals like *pesticides*, which are sprays that kills bugs, or *synthetic fertilizers*, which are chemicals added to the soil to make plants grow.

• Organic farmers use safer ways to control bugs and build the soil. This is important, because pesticides and synthetic fertilizers wash into rivers, lakes, and streams…and pollute them. They seep into the earth and pollute groundwater, too.

Answer: C. There are no pesticides on organic food.

- Pesticides and fertilizers harm animals, too. For example: In Costa Rica, pesticides from banana plantations get blown by wind into the rainforest, where they are pushing some frogs and other amphibians to extinction.

- Other chemicals you won't find in organic foods: *antibiotics*, *hormones*, *preservatives*, *artificial flavorings*, and *genetically engineered organisms*. What are these things? Look them up online. Lots of the foods we eat contain them.

- It's easy to tell when food is organic: It has the official U.S. Department of Agriculture (USDA) Organic label.

What You Can Do

- Try some organic food. Don't try to change all your eating habits at once. Try one or two organic foods—like bananas, since you know that helps animals. If you want, add more as time goes on.

- Grow an organic schoolyard! Get inspiration and help from the "Edible Schoolyard" program in Berkeley, CA. Watch this video: *edutopia.org/edible-schoolyard-video* and visit their web site: *edibleschoolyard.org/homepage.html*

Amaze Your Friends

They probably know there are lots of organic foods, but what about organic T-shirts?

That's right—there are T-shirts made from organic cotton. There are also organic

pajamas, blue jeans, shampoo, vitamins, sheets and blankets, pillows, pet food, candles, and toys. See if you can find 10 organic items in a store where you live...or look online: *green-shop.org/top-10-organic-products-online* or *tinyurl.com/6cxegt*

See for Yourself

• **Visit Ovie's Underground** from Organic Valley Family Farm: *oviesdigs.com*

• **Learn about organic farming** from Earthbound Farms Download the activity booklet: *ebfarm.com/justforkids*

• **It's science!** Try these cool science experiments about organics: *rodaleinstitute.org/science_experiments*

• **The inside story.** A game from Rainforest Alliance about growing bananas, chocolate, and coffee: *rainforest-alliance.org/education/treehouse/trackitback/index.html*

• **"My visit to a farm":** *ecokidsonline.com/pub/eco_info/ topics/landuse/organic_farm/index.cfm*

USING
ENERGY

WISELY

THOUGHTS ABOUT ENERGY

When I was a kid, my mom used to point out our power plant, a big brick building with three tall smokestacks and lots of big metal wires and machines outside of it. Inside, workers would feed coal to a big fire, and when the coal burned, it released energy that turned into electricity. At the same time, the coal released smoke into the air. As we drove past our power plant, my mom would point to the black smoke and say, "That's the dirtiest plant! We should close it down so it will stop polluting our air!" But back then we didn't know what we would do without the electricity.

We know a lot more now. We know that if we save enough energy, we'll still have electricity, but won't need as many power plants. And we know that there are other, cleaner ways to get electricity, like solar power and wind power.

We also know that the pollution coming from the plant doesn't just smell bad and make people sick, but it hurts the Earth, too. It is changing the weather all over the planet. Someday soon, wild animals might be too cold or too hot to survive. Our lives will change, too.

Already, some people are doing what they can to save energy so they can help clean up the dirty skies, streams, and land. And we are taking big steps toward renewable energy.

In this section you'll find lots of ways *you* can, too!

—Karina Lutz
Home Energy Magazine

35. GET A CHARGE FROM BATTERIES

Take a Guess:

Which of these doesn't need batteries?
A) A flashlight   B) A solar-powered calculator
C) A digital camera

You probably play with at least a few battery-operated toys, games, and other gizmos. After a while the batteries wear out, and you have to buy new ones, right?

What do you do with the old ones—just toss them out?

That's not good for the Earth. Those batteries contain dangerous chemicals that can leak into the ground. Plus, every time you throw out a battery, you use up precious resources.

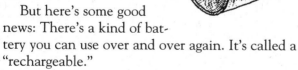

But here's some good news: There's a kind of battery you can use over and over again. It's called a "rechargeable."

Did You Know

• Americans buy *three billion* batteries every year. That's about 10 batteries for each person in the country—even including babies!

• Most of these batteries are made to be thrown away. But "rechargeable" batteries are made to be reused.

• How do they work? When they get run down, you put them into a little box called a *recharger*.

Answer: B. A solar-powered calculator gets its energy from the Sun.

• The recharger plugs into an electrical outlet. Then it takes electricity from the outlet and puts it into the battery.

• After being recharged for a while, the battery is ready to be used again.

• These batteries aren't perfect. But they're better for the Earth than disposable batteries. One rechargeable can take the place of up to 1,000 regular (single-use alkaline) batteries during its lifetime. Yep, that's *1,000!* Amazing, huh?

What You Can Do

Get the Most Out of Your Batteries

• Take batteries out of equipment that you're putting away for a while. Batteries might leak and ruin it.

• Don't put batteries (or things that have batteries in them) in a really hot place. Heat shortens a battery's life.

• Don't use old batteries with new ones. It wears out the new ones faster!

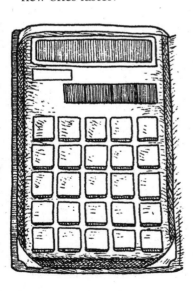

• Plug things in when you can. Or use equipment that doesn't need batteries at all, like a solar-powered calculator that runs on sunlight.

Try "Rechargeables"

• Talk to your parents about getting rechargeable batteries and a recharger.

• It costs more at first, but if you use lots of batteries, you'll actually *save* money in the long run.

Recycle Your Batteries

• Batteries—especially rechargeables—can be recycled.

• This is much better for the Earth, because we keep millions of batteries out of landfills, reuse some materials that went into making them, and cut pollution.

• Can you recycle batteries in your area? Go to *rbrc.org*, click on "Recycle Now," and enter your zip code where indicated. Or call 1-877-2RECYCLE (273-2925).

Amaze Your Friends

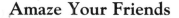

Ask them if they want some free batteries. Then tell them that one expert figured out that using rechargeables had saved him about $950! That's like getting about 475 batteries for free. To learn more visit: *greenlivingtips.com/articles/247/1/ Disposable-vs-rechargeable-batteries.html*

See for Yourself

• **Learn about different kinds of batteries:** *rbrc.org/consumer/education_kids.html* or *ehso.com/ehshome/ batteries.php#types*

• **Watch this:** *youtube.com/watch?v=VC8JhnDGAbk*

• **Lots of info:** *ehso.com/ehshome/batteries.php*

There's a lot more to see and do at **50simplekids.com**

36. LIGHTS OUT!

Take a Guess:
When was the first lightbulb invented?
A) Who knows?   B) Last year   C) Over 100 years ago

A t night when it gets dark, you flip a switch…and it's light again.

No big deal, right?

Think again. The energy that powers electric lights comes from the Earth. Being careful about using lights is another way we can help keep our planet healthy.

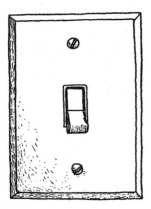

Did You Know

• Of all the energy that a regular lightbulb (called an *incandescent* bulb) uses, how much do you think is turned into light? Surprise! Only 1/10! The rest is *wasted*, because it is turned into heat instead. That's why a lightbulb is so hot after it's been on for a while.

• If a 100-watt bulb is on for half a day, every day, for a year, it can use enough electricity to burn almost 400 pounds of coal, which will release nearly 1,000 pounds of the gases that cause global warming!

• But here's good news: There's an amazing lightbulb called a "compact fluorescent" (CFL) that uses a 1/4 of the energy of a regular bulb and lasts 10 times as long.

• Experts say that if every American home replaced *just one* incandescent lightbulb with a compact fluorescent, we would save enough energy to light more than three million homes for a year…and keep 90 billion pounds of global

Answer: C. Thomas Edison invented it in 1879.

warming gases out of the air. Wouldn't it be great to put one (or more!) of them in your home?

What You Can Do

• Turn your lights out when you're not using them. Whenever you leave a room—and no one else is still there—be sure to flip the switch.

• Use daylight—it's free and doesn't pollute. If you're reading during the daytime, sit near a window. Open the curtain, or pull up the blinds or shades.

• Dust some lightbulbs, but make sure they're cool first. Believe it or not, dusty lightbulbs use more energy than clean ones. Ask your folks if you can help save energy (and keep the house clean, too) by dusting the lightbulbs once in a while.

• Go "bulb-shopping" with an adult. See if you can find compact fluorescent bulbs.

• Put CFLs in fixtures that are often on for more than 15 minutes a time, or several hours throughout the day.

Amaze Your Friends

Introduce them to the incredible *compact fluorescent*. They'll be astonished to find out how much of a difference one lightbulb can make! Go to *50simplekids.com/lights* to get the amazing facts about CFLs.

See for Yourself

- **"Turn the Lights Off!"** A game where you find all the lightbulbs and change them to CFLs: *touchstoneenergykids.com/ games/cfl_game.php*

- **"This Bulb."** See how changing a lightbulb can help fight global warming: *youtube.com/ watch?v=FvOBHMb6Cqc*

- **"Shining a New Light on Old Habits."** A good video to watch with your parents: *youtube.com/watch?v=t10D6Ud4RuU*

- Be an *Energy Hog Buster.* Fun site about saving energy. Kids only: *energyhog.org/childrens.htm*

- **Be an Energy Star!** Have fun saving energy: *energystar.gov/ index.cfm?c=kids.kids_index*

- **The Green Squad.** Save energy at school: *nrdc.org/ greensquad/library/lighting.asp*

There's a lot more to see and do at **50simplekids.com**

37. JOIN THE HEAT BUSTERS

Take a Guess:
Which of these is a good way to keep warm at home?
A) A match B) A sweater C) A hot tamale

Br-r-r. You're feeling chilly, so you walk over to the little dial that makes the heater work (the *thermostat*) and you turn it up.

Oh, no! Look out! You turned it up too far! You've just let out...*the Heat Monster!*

Here it comes, pouring out of the heater vents, eating up energy as it spreads around your home, making the air hotter and hotter.

But wait! There is something you can do to stop it.

Quickly you turn down the heat...and the Heat Monster disappears!

Congratulations! You've just joined the Heat Busters.

Did You Know

- Almost half of the energy you use in your home is spent on heating it.

- If all Americans turned their heat down 6° in the winter, we'd save the same amount of energy we get from 570,000 barrels of oil...*every single day.*

Answer: B. A sweater will keep you warm indoors, so you won't have to turn up the heat.

• Experts say the best temperature for your house is 65° to 68° F.

What temperature is *your* home in the winter?

• Here's more good news: Dialing down the thermostat *just 1°* during the winter can save 1% to 3% of your family's heating cost. That means you'll save a *lot* of money!

• When you use less oil for heat, you fight global warming. Every year, heating U.S. homes puts over a billion tons of the gases that cause global warming into the air. The easiest way to cut that down is by turning down the heat.

What You Can Do

• On cold days, keep the heat as low as you comfortably can.

• Instead of running around the house in a T-shirt and bare feet in winter—and turning up the heat to keep warm—you can help the Earth by dressing warmly. (Yes, even indoors.)

• When you go to sleep, try wearing warm pajamas and putting extra blankets on the bed. That way, you can turn the heat down at night and still stay comfortably warm.

• Do you have a furnace? Volunteer to help check the *air filter* with a grown-up. The filter is the screen that keeps dirt out of the furnace. If it gets clogged, your heater has to work harder—which means

it's using extra energy to keep you warm. An air filter has to be checked about once a month. It may need to be cleaned or replaced.

• By turning your thermostat down when you're not home—say, 10° or 15° for eight hours—you could save 10% a year on heating bills!

Amaze Your Friends

Tell them about these three ways people used to stay warm:

1) In the 1800s, people sometimes kept their hands warm by putting hot potatoes in their pockets.

2) To warm their beds, people used *hot water bottles*. See: *en.wikipedia.org/wiki/Hot_water_bottle*

3) In Australia, shepherds kept themselves warm at night by cuddling with dogs. A really cold night was called a *Three-Dog Night*. Makes you appreciate how lucky we are to have good heating, huh? So, let's take care of it!

See for Yourself

How warm is warm enough? Find out how low you can set your thermostat and still feel comfortable. Start by setting it 5° lower than usual, and put on a sweater or sweatshirt. If you get too warm after 10 or 15 minutes, turn the heat down another few degrees. On the other hand, if you're not warm enough (and putting on a heavier sweater doesn't do the trick), you can try setting the thermostat up just a degree or two. That's still several degrees lower than it was before!

38. STAY OUT OF HOT WATER

Take a Guess:
Where does the hot water in your house come from?
A) Clouds   B) Hot water factories   C) The water heater

If people from long ago saw our faucets, they'd say, "Hot water right out of the tap? Amazing!"

It used to take them a lot of time and energy to get hot water. People had to collect wood, light a fire, tend the fire …and then they *finally* had hot water!

What a difference it is today!

Now hot water is so easy to get that we let it run down the drain without even thinking. That's not a very good habit, because it still takes a lot of energy—though a different kind—to heat our water.

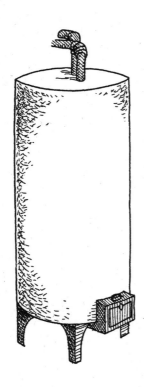

Did You Know

• The water supplied to your home is cold water—like the water in rivers, lakes, and wells, which is where household water comes from.

• A pipe carrying water to your home comes into the building and branches in two. One branch takes water to all the *Cold* faucets in your house. The other branch goes to the hot water heater, which in most homes is a big tank that holds

Answer: C. The water heater.

between 20 and 50 gallons. The heater goes on and stays on until the water gets hot.

• How does it know when to turn itself off? A little gadget called a *thermostat* checks the temperature and "tells" it.

• Now the hot water sits there, waiting to be used. When you turn the *Hot* faucet, hot water starts flowing out of the tank. It keeps flowing until you turn the faucet off.

• When hot water leaves the water heater, cold water takes its place. The thermostat "sees" that the water is getting too cold, so it turns on the heat again.

• This happens over and over, every day, even while you sleep: If the water gets cold, the heater turns on...even if no one is using hot water! It's easy to see why it takes so much energy to heat water!

What You Can Do

• We talked about not wasting water in Simple Thing #11, "Presto, On! Presto, Off!" Now we'll remind you to be a little extra careful when it comes to using hot water.

• By saving hot water, you save two treasures of the Earth at one time—water and energy.

• When you take a bath or a shower... when you wash your hands or face... when you're washing dishes... whenever you use hot water, remember: You have a chance to help save the Earth by using water wisely.

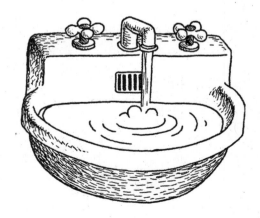

Take a Water Heater Safari

Ask an adult to set aside some time to look at your water heater with you. It's interesting to see… and you may discover some easy ways to save energy:

—*Check the water temperature.* You can save energy and still have hot water by turning it down to 120–130° F. Note: If your dishwasher doesn't have a separate heater, you may have to leave it at 140° F.

—*Feel the side of the water heater.* If it feels warm, some of the heat is escaping—which means it's wasting energy, and might need a special "insulating blanket" that you can get at a hardware store.

Amaze Your Friends

Show them these pictures of how people used to take baths:

* *website.lineone.net/~bill.sykes/019_Bath_in_front_of_Fire.jpg*
* *farm4.static.flickr.com/3282/2625212219_5240a14421.jpg?v=0*

Hard to believe, isn't it? In the old days, there were few water heaters. So hot water was a special treat—a luxury.

And if you think about it, it still is!

See for Yourself

* **Solar tale:** *sciencenewsfor kids.org/articles/20051109/ ScienceFairZone.asp*

39. IF IT'S NOT FAR, DON'T TAKE THE CAR

Take a Guess:
What do you think causes more pollution?
A) Fireplaces   B) Cars   C) Steamships

Need to go somewhere? Down to the store...over to a friend's house...out to a movie? The easiest thing to do is get a ride in the car.

But that's not the best thing for the Earth.

Cars create pollution, so the less we drive, the healthier our planet will be.

Sure, it may take you a little longer to get where you're going...but isn't clean air and water worth the extra effort?

Did You Know

• There are more cars in America than anywhere else in the world!

• Every year American cars drive three trillion miles. How many is that? Well, it would take you your whole life just to *count* that high!

Answer: B. Cars are some of the biggest polluters in the world!

- When these millions of cars burn up gas, they produce something called "exhaust"—it is one of the worst things for the Earth.

- Exhaust contains invisible gases like carbon dioxide and *nitrogen oxides* that add to global warming and air pollution.

- Bicycles don't make exhaust—they don't pollute. So, if you ride a bike, you're already saving the Earth.

What You Can Do

- Next time you go somewhere, think twice before you ask for a ride. Is it close enough to walk? Can you ride a bike?

- Encourage your parents to walk or bike instead of riding. Suggest that you can walk or bike *together*!

At School

- Talk to your teacher and principal about starting programs that promote walking and biking.

- At Sunnyvale Environmental School in Portland, Oregon, biking is a part of the curriculum. Watch their video: *youtube.com/watch?v=VYRX3NKtQ0A*

- Thousands of schools around the country participate in International Walk and Bike to School Day (*walknbike.org*) and Walk to School Day (*walktoschool.org*). How about yours?

Amaze Your Friends

• Show them Japan's incredible bicycle parking garage (*gizmodo.com/5046854/tokyos-robotic-bike-parking-garage-is-awesome*). Wouldn't it be great to have something like that in the United States someday?

See for Yourself

• **A short video about Walk to School Day:** *youtube.com/watch?v=ZOUiqubr_Fc*

• **Your bike helmet**—make sure you're wearing it the right way: *cpsc.gov/KIDS/kidsafety/correct.html*

• **Bike safety tips:** *www.nhtsa.dot.gov/people/injury/ pedbimot/bike/KidsandBikeSafetyWeb/index.htm*

• **The Green Guide:** *greenguideforkids.blogspot.com/ 2007/09/walk-bike-rollerskate-or-skateboard-to.html*

There's a lot more to see and do at **50simplekids.com**

40. STOP THE GREAT ESCAPE

Take a Guess:
Where does most heat escape from your house?
A) The telephone   B) The TV   C) The windows

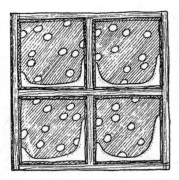

Right now, in your home, there's a great escape going on! Air is sneaking out around windows and doors—and in the winter, that's a crime! It costs us a lot to keep our homes warm. So, we've got to catch the air before it gets out.

Did You Know

• About 40% of the energy we use at home is for heat. And half of that is wasted!

• This means that with the energy we now spend heating our homes, we could actually heat *two* of them! It's true!

• How does the heat escape? Under doors, around window frames, through the attic, up the chimney…It can even go right through glass windows, especially if they're broken.

• By keeping even a little heat from being lost, you are helping fight global warming…and saving oil, coal, and other treasures of the Earth that get used for heat.

Answer: C. The cracks around windows and doors are big energy wasters.

What You Can Do

• Pull down the window shades at night and close the curtains when it's cold. This makes a "wall" that helps keep heat inside. Closing the curtains can save as much as 1/3 of the heat that would have escaped through the window.

• Make sure the windows in your room are closed tightly on cold nights. And make sure any broken windows get fixed!

• Plug the cracks around doors and windows.

—Make a *Door Draft Stopper*. That's something you put on the floor in front of a door, to keep cold air from coming in the crack at the bottom. It's easy to make. (See the next page for info on how to do it.)

—See if your parents are willing to put *weather stripping* around leaky doors and windows.

You may not have heard of this before, but you can find it at almost any hardware store. It doesn't cost much and it's pretty easy to install. Ask if you can help!

Amaze Your Friends

Take them on a "Leak Hunt" to see how many leaks there are in a normal house.

• On the next cold, windy day, take a 6-inch piece of ribbon or a piece of light paper around to all the windows and doors you want to check.

• Hold the ribbon or paper up to the places where the air might be escaping; whenever the ribbon or paper moves, you've found a leak.

• **Bonus:** Make a map showing the leaks and give it to your parents. What an eco-detective!

See for Yourself

• **Make a Door Draft Stopper.** There are lots of ways to do it. And they all work! Check out these sites. (You may need an adult to help you sew them.)

—*epa.state.il.us/kids/teachers/activities/draft-stopper.html*

—*jas.familyfun.go.com/arts-and-crafts?page=CraftDisplay&craftid=11565*

—*thriftyfun.com/tf957998.tip.html*

—*craftycrafty.tv/2007/09/how_to_make_your_own_dog_or_sn_1.html*

• **Find air leaks!** Some pointers: *powerhousekids.com/stellent2/groups/public/documents/pub/phtv_se_we_gs_000529.hcsp*

• **Plug leaky windows. Show your parents this site:** *waltonemc.com/Newsletter_Archive/2007_11_windows.htm*

There's a lot more to see and do at **50simplekids.com**

41. KEEP IT COOL

Take a Guess:
Which uses more electricity?
A) A radio B) A refrigerator C) Uncle Fester

What is an icebox? Back in the old days, before electricity and refrigerators, everyone had a box in the kitchen where they put a big hunk of ice. That's how they kept their food cold.

But didn't the ice melt? It sure did. So, every week an iceman came by to deliver more ice.

It wasn't nearly as easy as it is today. On the other hand, it didn't use up the Earth's resources the way refrigerators do.

So, do you think you can convince your parents to get rid of your refrigerator and get an icebox instead?

Ha! No way! But here are some things you *can* do with your refrigerator.

Did You Know

• We open our refrigerators almost 22 times a day. That's over 8,000 times a year for each one!

• When you open the refrigerator, the cold air you feel coming out is trading places with hot air going in. That means

Answer: B. Refrigerators are on all day, every day of the year! We never turn them off.

the fridge is getting warmer inside and has to use lots of extra electricity to cool back down.

• When a refrigerator is full of food, it needs less electricity to keep cold, because the food soaks up the cold air and keeps it trapped inside.

• There's a dial inside the fridge for adjusting its temperature. But many people don't know it, so refrigerators often end up colder than they need to be.

• The "coils"—those things that look like tubes—on the back or bottom of the fridge are important. They help keep your refrigerator cold by taking the heat out from the inside. But they don't work well when they're dusty.

What You Can Do

• Check the seal—the long rubber strip—on the edge of

the door. If there is food or dirt stuck in the seal, cold air might be escaping through it. You can stop that energy waste by cleaning the seal with a wet sponge.

• Don't open your refrigerator unless you have to. Once you've opened it, quickly get what you want and close the door. Think about what you want before you open it.

• If your folks say it's okay, make it your job to keep the coils free of dust. Brush the coils off with a broom, dustcloth, or (with their permission) a vacuum cleaner.

- With a parent's help, see if your refrigerator is colder than necessary. It should be set between 38° and 42° F.

Amaze Your Friends

Show them a quick trick that will tell them whether their refrigerator door seals are leaking or not. Close the door over a piece of paper or a dollar bill so it is half in and half out of the refrigerator. If you can pull the paper or bill out easily, the latch may need adjustment or the seal may need cleaning or replacing.

See for Yourself

- Keep a record of how many times you open the refrigerator during the day. Are you opening it more than you need to? And how long do you keep it open?

- To really appreciate your refrigerator, check out what people used to have, not too long ago.

  —**Icebox video.** Here's how the old iceboxes worked: *youtube.com/watch?v=Vid1sI-dKok*

  —**An old ad.** From 1926, showed in silent movies! *youtube.com/watch?v=qrNw3b5jrD4&feature=related*

  —**Old-fashioned refrigerators.** A great video that shows you what refrigerators used to look like. Long, but fun. *youtube.com/watch?v=EuXGX_i0etY&feature=related*

*There's a lot more to see and do at **50simplekids.com***

42. WHAT'S COOKING?

Take a Guess:
What is the fastest way to boil a pot of water?
A) Leave the lid on   B) Insult it   C) Make it angry

Congratulations! You're finally old enough to use the stove or microwave—your mom or dad said that you can turn it on by yourself!

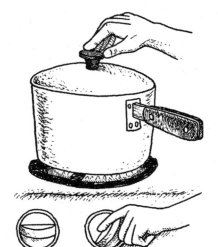

Stoves use a lot of energy. And when you're old enough to use the stove, you're also old enough to know how to save energy while using it.

What if you're still waiting for your folks to decide whether you're old enough? Well, in the meantime, you can teach *them* a few energy-saving cooking tips.

Did You Know

• Every time you open an oven door to see what's cooking, 25° to 50° of heat goes flying out the door. That's a lot!

• When hot air escapes from the oven, more electricity or gas is needed to heat the oven back up again. That means energy—and money—wasted.

• More than 90% of the homes in the U.S. have microwave ovens! Do you? If used properly, microwaves need a lot less energy than regular ovens. Toaster ovens use less energy than ovens, too.

Answer: A. Leaving the lid on creates heat much faster.

- A covered pot of water boils faster than an uncovered pot, so it uses less energy to reach the boiling point.

- You can use up to 25% less heat if you bake with glass or ceramic (clay) pans. They hold heat better than other pans.

What You Can Do

- Put a cover on your pot when you're boiling water.

- Use a microwave instead of a stove if you're defrosting, or cooking something small. Microwaves use about *50% less energy* than regular ovens! For big stuff, a stove is better.

- Keep your stovetop clean and shiny. When it stays shiny, it reflects heat up to the pot...which *saves* energy!

- Leave the oven door closed while you're baking.

- Listen to your food and pots while you are cooking. If you hear whistles, screams, loud sizzles, or other weird noises you're not used to, the heat may be turned up too high.

- For best results, the bottom of your pot should be the same size as the burner you're cooking on.

Amaze Your Friends

Demonstrate that if they boil water in a covered pot, they'll save energy.

Here's how:

1) Fill two pots with the same amount of water. (Measure it out with a measuring cup.)

2) Cover one pot; leave the other uncovered. Start the heat on both of them at the same time. Be sure the heat is set at the same level.

So which one will boil first? Answer: The one with the cover...because the heat stays in the pot. The water gets hotter faster—and that means you use less energy to make it boil. Simple, huh?

See for Yourself

• **12 tips on saving energy.** Not just for kids, but good info: *greenlivingtips.com/articles/252/1/Saving-energy-when-cooking.html*

• **More cooking tips:** *care2.com/greenliving/save-kitchen-energy-10-cooking-tips.html*

Cook with the Sun!

Save energy and amaze your friends by building a solar cooker. Talk to your teacher about making one in school:

• *pbskids.org/zoom/activities/sci/solarcookers.html*

• *aces.miamicountryday.org/SolarCookers/solar_cookers.htm*

43. UNPLUG IT!

Take a Guess:
If you want to save energy, what do you need to unplug?
A) Earplugs   B) A pair of shoes   C) An electric plug

U h-oh…Watch out! Vampires are hiding in your home: *Energy* vampires. They look harmless, but don't let that fool you—they suck power out of the Earth.

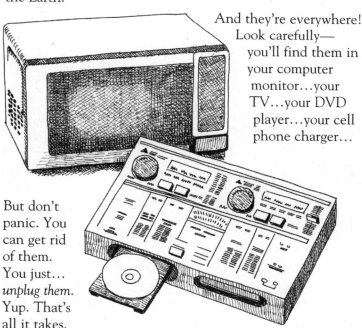

And they're everywhere! Look carefully— you'll find them in your computer monitor…your TV…your DVD player…your cell phone charger…

But don't panic. You can get rid of them. You just… *unplug them.* Yup. That's all it takes.

Did You Know

• Some electronics secretly use energy just because they're plugged in—even when they're turned off, and you're not using them.

Answer: C. Unplug electronic devices when they're not being used!

- This is called *standby power*. It's built into things with remote controls, like TVs and stereos. And it's hiding in things with digital displays—like the clock on your microwave or DVD player.

- Other hidden energy vampires: Battery chargers for things like cell phones (when you leave them plugged in) and anything with an *external power supply* (those big black boxes), like computers and MP3 players.

- Vampires are tricky! For example: Believe it or not, your microwave oven uses *more* electricity to power its digital clock than it does to cook! Even though heating food uses 100 times more power than it takes to run the clock, microwave ovens are turned off most of the time, while their clocks glow *all* of the time.

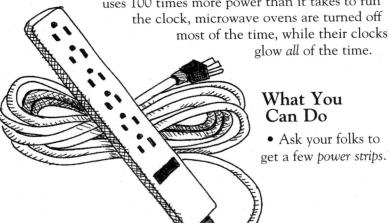

What You Can Do

- Ask your folks to get a few *power strips*.

You plug a bunch of things into a power strip at the same time...and then you can turn them off all at once. Just flip the switch at night when you go to bed, and turn them on again in the morning.

- Go exploring: There are "smart" power strips that turn off *some* devices automatically, but *leave* ones you need on.

- Unplug kitchen appliances that your family only uses sometimes—like blenders, microwaves, and coffeemakers.

- Unplug electronics like TVs, DVD players, gaming consoles, and stereos, plus computers (especially the monitors) and printers when they're not being used.

- Once you've charged your MP3 player, cell phone, digital camera, cordless toothbrush, or battery, unplug the charger!

Amaze Your Friends

Take them on a safari, hunting for energy vampires. According to one study, a typical American home has 20 electrical appliances that use power even when they're turned off. What about your house...and your friends' homes? Find out! How many are there? Which ones can be turned off safely when they're not being used?

See for Yourself

- **Stop the energy vampires** with PBS Kids' *The Greens*: *meetthegreens.pbskids.org/episode5/energy-vampires.html*

- **Professor Questor** will show you how much energy vampires use, and give you tips on what to unplug: *energyquest.ca.gov/vampires/dswmedia/index.html*

- **Screensavers waste energy!**
Download this invisible screensaver instead: *usefulscreensaver.com.au*

44. SUN POWER!

Take a Guess:
How long does it take for sunlight to get to Earth?
A) A million years   B) 50 years   C) Around 8 minutes

I magine turning on a light switch…and finding that all the electricity has been used up.

Could this really happen? It's possible. Most of the energy we use now comes from sources such as oil and coal that will run out some day. They're called *nonrenewable* energy sources, because when they're gone, there's no way to replace them. On top of that, they're a main source of global warming gases and pollution.

But there are other sources of energy we could be using that *are* renewable. They won't run out, and they're better for the Earth because they pollute less—or not at all.

Did You Know

• One of the best sources of renewable energy is the Sun. Every day it sends energy to the Earth in the form of heat and light. This is called *solar energy*.

• Believe it or not, some people already use solar energy to heat water and buildings, make electricity, and run cars.

Answer: C. And it travels 93 million miles!

- Scientists expect that sometime soon, many more people will get their everyday power from the Sun!

- The wind is another energy source that will last forever. It is the world's fastest-growing type of renewable energy.

- Electricity is made when wind is captured by a *turbine*, which looks like a giant fan. Hundreds of wind turbines, side by side, are called a *wind farm*. They can provide electricity for a whole town!

- Some other kinds of renewable energy sources are *biomass*, made from plants; *hydropower* that uses moving water in oceans or rivers; and *geothermal*, which gets power from the heat deep inside the Earth itself.

What You Can Do

- Learn all you can about renewable energy. Talk about it with your family, friends, and class. By spreading the word, you're helping this new kind of energy to grow, because most Americans don't understand how *real* it is. They think it's still just make-believe!

- Send letters to the editor of your local newspaper (Simple Thing #46), and e-mails to your congressperson (Simple Thing # 49). Tell them we need alternative energy now!

See for Yourself

• **"Wind with Miller"** is an interactive site from the Danish Wind Industry! You can even build your own wind turbine: *www.windpower.org/en/kids/index.htm*

• **Solar facts!** Questions and answers about solar energy, just for kids, from Solar Energy International (SEI): *solarenergy.org/resources/youngkids.html*

• **Read this!** "The Energy Story" from the State of California's Energy Quest web site for info on all kinds of energy sources: *energyquest.ca.gov/story/index.html*

• **Explore for energy.** The U.S. Energy Information Administration's (EIA) kids' page: *eia.doe.gov/kids/ energyfacts/sources/whatsenergy.html*

• **Solar oven.** A solar oven made from a recycled pizza box, but not just for cooking pizza! Needs some adult help: *solarnow.org/pizzabx.htm* (See page XXX, too.)

• **Roofus the Dog.** Visit Roofus's solar and energy efficient home. (Learn how to build a sundial, too!): *www1.eere.energy.gov/kids/roofus/*

There's a lot more to see and do at **50simplekids.com**

SPREADING

THE WORD

SPREAD
THE WORD

It's great to learn how to take action on our own. The truth is, we can get things done just because we *want* to! But it's just as important to reach out to other people… because the other truth is, we have a lot *more* power when we work together.

This is one of the big keys to saving the Earth. So, use all that kid-power! When you write a letter to your senator that says, "Put money into solar energy! I want to have clean electricity when I grow up!" show it to your friends. They'll want to write to their senator, too.

When you get interested in organic food, organize a trip to a farm, so you and your friends or family can share the experience. When you want to learn more about climate change, ask your teacher a question. Other kids will want some answers, too. And when your friends tell you what they're doing to spread the word, help them by spreading it too.

Whether you're working with your classmates, your family, or people in the government, you'll have a great new feeling when you realize you're on the same team— exploring the world together, trying to save energy together, looking for leaks together…and sharing your thoughts and feelings about the most important issue there is: saving the Earth.

45. IT'S A FAMILY AFFAIR

Take a Guess:
Do parents care about the Earth?
A) *Of course* B) *Only on Tuesdays* C) *No, they're too old*

Psstt! Want to know a secret? Your parents really care what you think...even though they sometimes pretend not to.

So here's a chance to help save the Earth by getting *them* involved, too.

When families work together to protect the planet, they can accomplish a whole lot...and they can have a lot of fun at the same time. It can make a family closer, too, because you're sharing something very important. And let's face it—there are some things kids just can't do by themselves. You need help!

Did You Know

• When your parents were kids, hardly anyone ever worried about saving the environment. That's because they didn't know it was in trouble.

• They developed some habits that aren't good for the environment: They made as much garbage as they wanted; they wasted energy whenever they wanted; they used up the Earth's treasures just for fun.

Answer: A. Of course they do!

• Today we all know better—but it's hard for grown-ups to change the way they do things. You can make the difference by giving them a reason to try harder.

• Besides that, your parents might not even know about the problems facing the Earth! So, when you talk to them about saving it, you might be doing them a big favor.

• But remember that you can't do everything. Some projects cost money, and your parents have to work on other things, too. So, you'll probably have to decide which things are *most* important. That's called *setting priorities*.

What You Can Do

• Do some research to see which things your family can do. Remember to keep track of how much things will cost... and *how much money you can save*. That could be a big part of deciding which things they want to do.

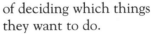
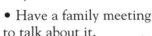

• Have a family meeting to talk about it.

• Be creative and have fun! Make an organic breakfast together, pick a place to volunteer for a day (like a stream clean-up or a wildlife refuge), switch lightbulbs one at a time, and so on.

Amaze Your Friends

Trust us—when they see you and your family working together, they'll be amazed. And maybe it will inspire them to try to get *their* families involved, too. We can always hope!

See for Yourself

• **A checklist for your family:** *food-home.kaboose.com/ go-green-checklist.html*

• **A great starting point:** *ecologue.com*

• **Oprah's ideas:**
oprah.com/article/world/environment/green_living_dunne

• **Green activities:** *ehow.com/how_4562018_do-green-activities-kids.html*

• **How to Green Your Parents:**
green101.experience.com/2008/11/green-your-parents.html

• **10 ways to go green:** *canadianparents.com/article/ 10-tips-to-help-your-family-go-green*

There's a lot more to see and do at **50simplekids.com**

46. MAKE NEWS

Take a Guess:
Which of these is the easiest to write an e-mail with?
A) A piece of chalk   B) A computer   C) A hammer

Extra! Extra! Read all about it!
Where? In the newspaper…and online, at a newspaper's web site.
Would you like to tell everyone what you think about saving the Earth? Why not write a letter or e-mail to your local newspaper?

Did You Know

• Every day about 1/3 of all Americans read a newspaper, either in print or online.

• Most daily newspapers have a special section called "Letters to the Editor." These letters are written to the newspapers by readers who have ideas they want to share.

• The newspapers print the letters because they feel it is important for people to voice their opinions.

• Usually, the letters are written by adults. But every once in a while, a kid will write. When that happens, people pay extra attention to it, because kids have a special way of looking at the world.

Answer: We're not telling. But please don't try to write an e-mail with a hammer.

What You Can Do
At Home

• Write a letter to your local paper. Tell them what you're doing to save our world. Or, tell them what you wish everyone would do—and why.

• Start with "Dear Editor." And when you finish it, be sure to add your name, address, and phone number. They won't print that, but they need to know how to find you so they can be sure you really sent the letter.

• Most Letters to the Editor are now sent as e-mails, rather than through the mail.

• Ask an adult to help you get the newspaper's online address. Usually you can find it on the "Letters to the Editor" page of the paper or on their web site.

• If the newspaper doesn't print your letter, don't give up. Keep writing. The more times you write, the more chances there are that one of your letters will be printed.

• If that happens, many people will be able to read it. And they'll learn something important about saving the Earth.

At School

• Suggest to your teacher that your class could write to the local newspaper...or a national newspaper, like *USA Today*. Why not?

• Your class can have a discussion about saving the Earth.

Then you can write a group letter together and sign it "From the ___ class at ___ school" (fill in the blanks with your grade and school name).

Or each person can write her or his own letter and your class can send them all together.

Amaze Your Friends

Make your own "Save the Earth" *YouTube* video. Send the web link to everyone you know. Send it in a letter to the local newspaper, too! Maybe they'll even write a story about it.

See for Yourself

• **How to write a letter to the editor.** Here's one person's advice: *associatedcontent.com/article/137491/the_ultimate_guide_to_getting_a_letter.html?page=1&cat=9*

There's a lot more to see and do at **50simplekids.com**

47. GO "GREEN"
AT SCHOOL

Where can you start working to change the world?

Why not at your school? That's one place where you know they'll listen to kids. And since schools spend *billions* of dollars every year on paper, books, and other supplies...use lots of water and energy...and use plenty of chemicals for cleaning and landscaping, changing anything they do can have a *really* big impact!

Think about it: Wouldn't it be great if your school was the "greenest" it could possibly be?

Not only would you be helping to save the Earth, but you'd also be helping your classmates, teachers, and even the staff at school to become healthier!

Answer: C. A "green" school is committed to making the Earth a top priority!

Did You Know

There are many ways your school can be green. Here are a few:

• **Buy recycled paper, and products made of recycled materials, for every class.** It's not enough just to recycle paper—we have to buy the products made of recycled materials, too!

• **Always use both sides of the paper** when making copies (to save paper).

• **Don't let buses and cars "idle"** (let the engine run) in parking lots and driveways. If someone's going to wait for more than 30 seconds, they should turn their engine off. Cars and buses give off a lot of global-warming pollution.

• **Buy nontoxic paint and cleaning products.** About 53 million kids spend at least six hours a day in school, 180 days a year. Many are exposed to indoor pollutants from paint and cleaners that have been tied to serious illnesses.

• **Cut energy use** by switching to compact fluorescents, turning lights off, and heating efficiently. The Little Rock, Arkansas, school system used 1,500 students in their "Energy Patrol" program and saved more than $700,000 dollars in energy costs in a year!

• **Reduce or completely stop using pesticides on school grounds.** Tests show that American kids from age 6 to 11 have more pesticides in their bodies than any other age group!

What You Can Do

• Get together a group of kids who want to help make your school green.

• Have a meeting with your teacher or principal to find out what's really possible at your school. What can your group do to help make it happen?

• Put together an "eco-fact sheet" with your group or class, and pass it around the school so kids will know how to help. Put it on recycled paper!

• Keep track of the changes and the money that's saved. Send a letter about it to the editor at your local paper!

See for Yourself

Some sites to check out:
• *www.greenschools.net/7StepstoaGreenSchool.htm*
• *eco-schools.org/aboutus/howitworks.htm*
• *greenschoolproject.com/*
• *www.deq.state.or.us/lq/education/*
• *ase.org/greenschools/start.htm*
• *www.recycleworks.org/schools/s_audits.html*

There's a lot more to see and do at **50simplekids.com**

48. TAKE A FIELD TRIP

Take a Guess:
What's a field trip, anyway?
A) You meet Mrs. Fields B) You learn how to field a baseball
C) You take a trip to see something in person

There's a lot to learn about the Earth and the way we live on it. Some things you can pick up on your own. Some you can learn from books and movies. But *some* things are easiest to understand when you go out and see them.

That's why we make special trips, called *field trips*, to the places where things are happening.

The places you visit to learn about our Earth might be very unusual or far away—like a wildlife refuge or an animal shelter. But they might also just be down the street, or right in the schoolyard...because interesting things are happening everywhere around us.

We can take field trips with our class in school...with our family...or sometimes just with our friends. But every time, the goal is the same: to see and experience something in a new way, and to help us learn.

Answer: C. You take a trip to see or do something special.

Did You Know

There are plenty of fascinating places in your community to visit.

Many of them welcome group visits and are glad to give tours— especially to schools!

For example:

- A water utility
- A wildlife refuge
- A recycling center
- An aquarium or zoo
- A science museum
- A local farm
- A landfill
- A wind farm

There are other places you can explore by yourself, or with a teacher: wetlands, a field (that would be a field-field trip, wouldn't it?), a garden, a stream, and so on.

How to Plan a Field Trip

1) *Investigate*

- If it's a school trip, talk to your teachers. Let them know you're willing to do some investigating about the places you might go.

- Make a list of interesting places in your community that have an environmental connection. Whenever possible, look up the places' phone numbers and write them on the list.

- Show the list of places to your teacher(s). Together, pick out a couple of good possibilities for a field trip. Then your teacher can call these places to find out if it would be okay for your class to visit.

2) *Help find a way to pay for the trip*

• Renting a bus to go on a field trip can be pretty expensive, so your class may need to raise money to pay for it.

• One way to do that: Have an aluminum can drive at your school. Or a garage sale. Or ask the PTA to help.

• If your class can't raise enough money to go on a field trip, have the field trip come to you. Ask an expert on alternative energy, someone from your recycling center, or someone from an environmental group to come talk to your class. Usually that doesn't cost any money at all.

See for Yourself

• **The "Rotten Truth."** How to organize a landfill field trip: *astc.org/exhibitions/rotten/tour.htm*

• **"Let's Go to the Zoo!"** A video about a trip to the zoo in Portland, Oregon: *youtube.com/watch?v=ryI7jCmth40*

• **One example.** Field trip programs in the Arboretum in Flagstaff, Arizona: *thearb.org/field.htm*

There's a lot more to see and do at **50simplekids.com**

49. GET INVOLVED

Take a Guess:
Which of these is an environmental group?
A) The Sierra Club B) The New York Yankees
C) The Jonas Brothers

T he goal of this book is to show you that you have the power to make a difference: You can do things all by yourself that will change the world.

But sometimes that's not enough. To make even bigger things happen, people need to join forces and work together. Ten people…a hundred people…a thousand people all working for the same thing can change the world in ways that just one person can't.

The trick is figuring out who to work with. Here are two good ideas:

Answer: A. The Sierra Club has been working to save the Earth for many years.

1. Work with elected officials.

People who are elected to the government represent many citizens. We give them a lot of power to make big changes.

• They can pass laws that help or hurt the Earth. And when they have to decide what law to pass, they listen to the people who elected them. That means you and everyone in your community.

• How can you talk to them? Elected officials pay attention to letters, phone calls, and e-mails. You probably won't talk to them directly, but you can call or write their local offices. The people who work there will pass your message on.

• You can find the phone number of a local official's office in the *government* pages of your phone book. Or go online.

• To find out how to reach your members of Congress in Washington, D.C.: *c-span.org/resources/*

• Be sure of what you want to say before you contact them. Talk about just one issue—not a whole bunch. And try to tell them what you're *for*, not what you're against.

2. Join forces with an environmental group.

• There are groups for almost anything you can think of. animals, global warming, soil, mining.

• Many groups have letter-writing campaigns and send "alerts" to people who sign up. They work hard talking to elected officials, trying to change the way people think. And they have very interesting web sites. Check them out! You can find many more at **50simplekids.com**:

• Natural Resources Defense Council: *nrdc.org*

• Friends of the Earth: *foe.org*

• Seacology: seacology.*org*

• Rainforest Action Network: *ran.org*

• Union of Concerned Scientists: *ucsusa.org*

• Sierra Club: *sierraclub.org*

• Earth Island Institute: *earthisland.org*

• Greenpeace: *greenpeace.org*

• Defenders of Wildlife: *defenders.org*

• The National Audubon Society: *audubon.org*

• The National Wildlife Federation: *nwf.org*

50. DREAM A BETTER WORLD

By Sophie Javna, age 15

One of the best parts of being a kid is dreaming about the future. What will I be when I grow up? A doctor? An astronaut? Will I get married and have children? Every kid has a different fantasy, but we all hope that whatever happens, it will be exciting and fun! Personally, I want to be a singer when I grow up—have my own band, record a CD, and maybe even sing at concerts.

My perfect future sounds great...until I come back to Earth and start thinking seriously about what the world will be like 10 or 20 years from now. Will there be lots of pollution?...Will animals like polar bears and elephants be extinct?...Will our beautiful rainforests be gone forever?

When I start thinking about that, I get scared that children all over the world won't have the lives they dream about...and that makes me really sad.

We all deserve to live on a beautiful planet with clean air, clear water, and safe food...and that's what we'll have if we stay focused on making our dreams come true. This is our world, the one we'll be living in when we're adults! It's our responsibility to start taking care of it *now*.

I know that we can do it! Start trying the things in this book. You'll feel so proud of yourself for doing something that has such an important and lasting impact, you'll make it a part of your life forever.

And *that's* what will make the difference!

ECO-

EXPERIMENTS

Eco-Experiment #1
BACK TO THE EARTH

Some things are "biodegradable"—which means they eventually break down and go back to the Earth. But which things are, and which aren't? This will help you figure it out.

What You'll Need
- An apple core
- A leaf of lettuce
- Some plastic packaging
- A piece of Styrofoam
- A small shovel

What to Do
1. Find a spot where it's OK to dig a few holes.

2. Dig four holes. Each one should be wide and deep enough to put something in.

3. Put the apple core in one hole, the lettuce in the next, the plastic in another, and the Styrofoam cup in the fourth hole.

4. Fill the holes back in with dirt.

5. Mark the spots where you've buried your four things. Make sure you'll be able to find them again.

6. Wait one month, then go back and dig them up.

7. You'll have no trouble finding the plastic and Styrofoam, but the lettuce and maybe the piece of apple will be gone.

What You Discover

• The lettuce and apple core are biodegradable; they can become part of the Earth again. They're in the soil where they can help grow more apples or grass or lettuce (Note: depending on where you dug your holes, it may take longer for the apple and lettuce to turn into soil. The warmer and moister the ground is, the quicker it will happen.)

• But the plastic packaging and Styrofoam are still there. They are made from the Earth's resources, but we have changed them into something that cannot become part of the Earth again.

• Which of these is better for us...and our planet? Are we taking too many things out of the Earth that can't be put back? Is it important for us to change?

Eco-Experiment #2

IT CAME FROM UNDERGROUND

We talked about pure, fresh underground water becoming polluted. Here's a demonstration of what can happen to us—and other living things—when it does.

What You'll Need

- A glass of water
- A stick of fresh celery with the leaves still on it
- Some red or blue food coloring

What to Do

1. Carefully cut off the bottom of the celery.

2. Put a couple of drops of food coloring into the glass. Pretend that this is pollution. Watch it spread out in the glass until all the water turns the same color. That's how pollution spreads.

3. Put the celery in the glass. Pretend that this is a little plant, a tree, or even a person who drinks water from the ground. Let the celery stalk sit there for a few hours.

4. After a few hours, go back and check out the celery. Cut it and you'll be able to see how the "polluted" water has moved up through the stalk.

What You Discover

• By "polluting" the water, we also "polluted" the plant. Clearly, whatever we do to our water, we do to ourselves and all other living things. A plant that gets its water from the ground will also drink the pollution in the water; a person who gets his or her water from the ground also is exposed to pollution. Because we can't avoid it, we have to prevent it.

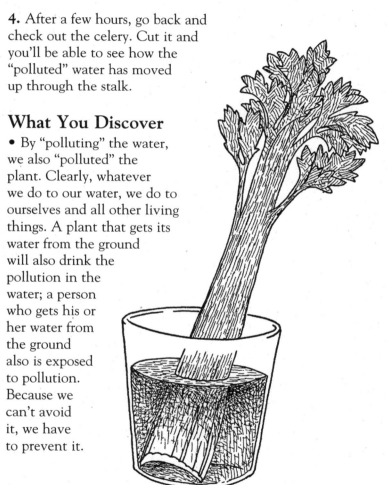

Eco-Experiment #3
SMOG PATROL

It's easy to talk about air pollution, but much harder to imagine what it's doing to things, plants, and people. This experiment will help you see what it actually does.

What You'll Need
- Eight natural rubber bands
- Two coat hangers
- A large plastic bag
- A magnifying glass

What to Do

1. Bend each coat hanger into a rectangle.

2. Slide four rubber bands onto each coat hanger, making sure they're stretched tight. If they're not tight at first, bend the coat hangers until they are.

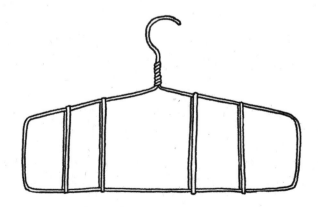

3. Hang one up outside in a shady place so it's out of the sun. That's important.

4. Put the other coat hanger in a plastic bag, and seal it tightly. Keep it indoors in a drawer.

5. Wait a week.

6. When a week is up, check out the rubber bands you hung outside. Are they cracked and broken? Use the magnifying glass to look over them carefully.

7. Compare the rubber bands you hung outside with the ones you kept in the bag, by stretching each group the same distance. Do you notice any difference?

8. If the rubber bands from outdoors are still in good shape, hang them back up for a few more weeks. See what happens to them over a longer time.

What You Discover

If you live in a place where the air is clean, it will take a long time for rubber bands to show damage. But if you live in an area where the air is very polluted, the rubber bands will break in a few weeks. That's because, unseen by you, smog—air pollution—has been eating away at them.

Polluted air is bad for all things on the Earth. It hurts animals, trees, farmers' crops, and even people, in the same way it damaged your rubber bands. That's why we need to stop it.

Eco-Experiment #4

RAINDROPS KEEP FALLING ON MY HEAD

*Invisible gases from power plants and cars sometimes mix with
water and make it "acidic," like vinegar. When these gases get
into rain clouds, they mix with rain or snow and the acid falls
back to Earth in the water. This is called "acid rain." Here
you'll see what this type of pollution can do to plants.*

What You'll Need
- Three 1-quart jars with lids
- Measuring cups
- Three small potted plants that you are willing to sacrifice in the name of science
- A bottle of vinegar or lemon juice
- Six short strips of masking tape to use as labels
- A pen or marker

What to Do

1. Make two labels that say "a little acid."

2. Measure 1/4 cup vinegar or lemon juice into one jar and fill it up the rest of the way with cold water from the tap.

3. Put one of the labels that says "a little acid" on the jar. Put the other one on one of the pots. You will use the mixture in this jar to water this plant.

4. Make two labels that say "a lot of acid." Repeat steps 2 and 3, but this time put a full cup of vinegar or lemon juice in the jar.

5. Write "tap water" on the last two labels. Put one on the last pot and the other on the last jar. Fill the last jar just with water.

6. Set the plants next to each other so they get the same amount of sunlight.

7. Whenever the plants need water (every 2–4 days), water each one with water from the jar that matches its label. See how long it takes for the effects of the acid to set in. What do you notice about the plants? How do they differ in color?

What You Discover

The more acid in the plant water, the sooner the plant dies. This is an illustration of what happens in nature when acid rain falls. It happened faster in your experiment than in nature, because you watered your plants with a stronger acid than most of the rain that falls in this country. (That way, you could see the results faster.) But rain is becoming more acidic all the time. We need to keep it from getting worse.

Eco-Experiment #5

BE A JUNK-FOOD DETECTIVE

When you go to your favorite fast-food restaurant and order a burger and French fries, do you think about what comes with them? We don't mean the pickles, onions, and special sauce—we mean the wrappers, bags, and other things you'll throw away. Let's take a look.

What You'll Need

- A few friends
- Some money to buy lunch
- A list of fast-food restaurants you can walk or ride your bike to.

What to Do

1. To do this experiment right you'll need to get fast food from several restaurants.

- To make this easy (and as cheap as possible), each person in your group will buy her or his lunch at a different restaurant.

- Buy about the same thing at each restaurant. Then you can really compare sandwiches with sandwiches, cold drinks with cold drinks, and desserts with desserts.

2. Okay, now go buy the food. Take it with you from restaurant to restaurant, but keep the food from each restaurant separate.

3. After you go to the last restaurant, take all the bags of food home and eat lunch. But don't throw the paper wrapping, cups, napkins, salt, plastic forks or spoons, Styrofoam hamburger carton, french fry containers, and all the other garbage away. Put it aside and—this is important—keep the stuff you got from each restaurant separate.

4. Now sort through it all. Figure out which restaurants sold the most garbage with your lunch. Figure out which ones sold you the least. Are you surprised at how much there is? Imagine that millions of people buy the same food—and get the same garbage—every single day. What a mess! What a waste!

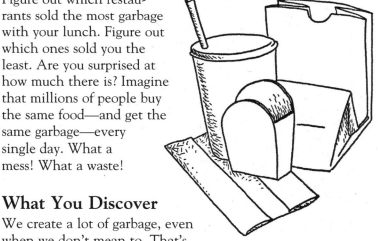

What You Discover

We create a lot of garbage, even when we don't mean to. That's one of the big reasons we're running out of places to put it. But what can we do about it?

Well, we could stop eating at fast-food restaurants.

But what if we like fast food? What do we do then?

Maybe we could just go to fast-food restaurants that sell us the least garbage, or that recycle it.

But what if those restaurants aren't our favorites? What do we do then?

You see, it's not always easy to decide what to do. In order to save the Earth, we often have to make tough choices. But then...what other choice do we have if we really care?

Eco-Experiment #6
THINKING BEYOND

Why is it so hard for us to take care of the Earth? Maybe we are so concerned with our own lives that we just don't pay attention to other important things. This experiment will help you explore that idea.

What You'll Need
• Some friends
• A big square piece of paper (three feet long and three feet wide would be good)
• A pencil and a small piece of paper for each person

What to Do
1. Lay the big sheet of paper on the floor. Draw lines and labels on it so it looks like the picture below.

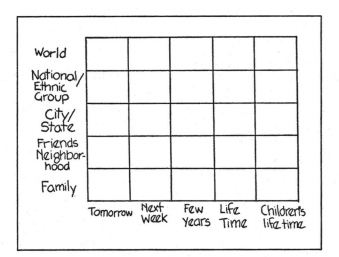

2. Ask your friends to decide where they do their "best thinking." For example: Is it in bed, just before they fall asleep? Or when they're riding their bikes? Or in the shower? When they've each figured it out, you're ready for the next step.

3. Ask your friends to close their eyes and imagine a time last week when they were doing their "best thinking."

4. Now ask each of them to write down 10 things they were thinking about doing at that time, and when they were thinking about doing them. For example: Were they thinking about eating dinner that night? Or seeing friends on Saturday? Or going to the movies next week?

5. It's time for the big sheet of paper.

• Everyone puts a mark in the boxes where each of their 10 thoughts belongs. For example: If they were thinking about going to the movies with their friends next week, they put a mark in the box where "Next Week" and "Friends" meet (as the drawing below shows).

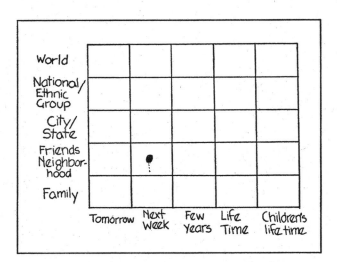

6. Now everyone should step back and take a look at where the dots are.

What You Discover

Almost everybody's thoughts center on the things that are closest to us—our family and friends, our neighborhoods and schools, and events that will happen soon.

See how we're not used to thinking about the environment? Even if we care about saving the Earth, we hardly ever think about it. But with some practice, we can!

• We can think about the Earth while we're brushing our teeth, and then turn off the faucet to save water.

• We can think about the Earth when we want to go someplace, and then get on our bikes—or walk—instead of getting our parents to drive us in a car.

• We can turn off lights when we're not using them, knowing we are helping save energy.

• We can make the *50 Simple Things* a part of our lives just by thinking about the Earth every single day!

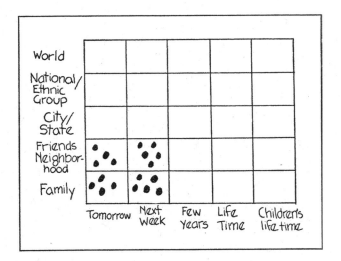

Eco-Experiment #7

MAKE YOUR OWN RECYCLED PAPER

The best way to learn how recycled paper is made is…to make it yourself! This is from First Steps to Ecology, *a book printed by the Ecology Center in Berkeley, California.*

What You'll Need

- Two and one-half single pages from a newspaper
- A whole section of a newspaper
- A blender
- Five cups of water
- A big square pan that's at least three inches deep
- A piece of window screen that fits inside the pan
- A measuring cup
- A flat piece of wood the size of a newspaper's front page

What to Do

1. Tear the 2-1/2 pages of newspaper into tiny pieces.

2. Drop the pieces into the blender.

3. Pour five cups of water into the blender.

4. Cover the blender. (You don't want to have to scrape newspaper mush off the walls!)

5. Switch the blender on for a few seconds, or until the paper is turned into pulp.

6. Pour about one inch of water into the pan.

7. Pour the blended paper (pulp) into a measuring cup.

8. Put the screen into the pan.

9. Pour one cup of blended paper pulp over the screen.

10. Spread the pulp evenly in the water with your fingers. Feels mushy, doesn't it?

11. Lift the screen and let the water drain.

12. Open the newspaper section to the middle.

13. Place the screen with the pulp into the newspaper.

14. Close the newspaper.

15. Carefully flip over the newspaper section so the screen is on top of the pulp. This step is very important!

16. Place the board on top of the newspaper and press to squeeze out excess water.

17. Open the newspaper and take out the screen.

18. Leave the newspaper open and let the pulp dry for at least 24 hours.

19. The next day, check to make sure the pulp paper is dry.

20. If it is, carefully peel it off the newspaper.

21. Now you can use it to write on!

What You Discover

See how easy it is to make recycled paper? Now that you know how easy it is, you can help save trees and fight the garbage problem by recycling your paper...and buying recycled paper.

QUICK

QUIZZES

QUICK QUIZ #1:
USING ENERGY

*Let's see how much you and your friends know about
using—and saving—energy. Answers start on page 205.*

1) True or false: Every year America uses less energy,
because we all know how important it is to save energy.

2) Of all the big appliances in your home, which one generally uses the most energy?
 a) A dishwasher   b) A refrigerator   c) A washing machine

3) If you want to save energy at home, it's a good idea to…
        a) Tiptoe around your house   b) Turn down the heat
                    c) Chew sugar-free gum

4) Most global warming pollution in the world is caused
by using energy. Take a guess: Which energy-user produces
more global warming pollution—your car or your home?

5) True or false: An average house has so many little places
that cold air can come in, it's the same as having a big hole
in the wall.

6) True or false: Switching to electric cars is a good way to
save energy.

7) True or false: Solar energy is a good idea, but we can't
really count on the Sun to help solve our energy problems.

8) What is an Energy Star appliance?
   a) A dishwasher owned by a rock star   b) A stove that's
   shaped like a star   c) An appliance that's energy-efficient

9) What happens if you put in a compact fluorescent lightbulb instead of a regular bulb?
        a) You start laughing   b) You save a lot of energy
                    c) Your house melts

QUICK QUIZ #2:
USING WATER

Now for our next quiz. Let's see what kind of water experts you and your friends are. Answers start on page 205.

1) In what room do we use the most water?

a) The kitchen   b) The bathroom   c) The laundry room

2) True or false: The average American family turns on the tap about 50 times a day.

3) Imagine that every drop of water in the world fits into a little one-gallon jug. Now, how much of that water do you think would be fresh water you can drink?

a) Just one tablespoon   b) Enough to fill a soda can
c) Enough to fill a cereal bowl

4) You know that we need fresh water to live, right? So how long do you think you could you live without drinking it?

a) About 5 minutes   b) About a week   c) About a month

5) True or false: Most people in places like Africa and Asia are like you, and get their drinking water from a faucet in their bathroom or kitchen.

6) True or false: For about one billion people in the world, drinking water is very dangerous—the only water they can get often makes them very sick and sometimes causes death.

7) People in some countries use a lot less water than in others. In India, for example, the average person uses only about 14 gallons of water every day. In Germany, it's about 47 gallons a day. How many gallons do you think the average (like you) American uses each day?

a) About 10   b) About 96   c) About 175

QUICK QUIZ #3:
PROTECTING ANIMALS

*Quiz #3 is about saving animals. Are you an animal
expert? Let's find out. Answers start on page 205.*

1) True or false: The Endangered Species Act already protects too many animals. We should stop adding more animals to the "endangered" list.

2) Why is it dangerous for animals if you throw food out of the window of your car?
   a) It might hit them in the eye b) It makes them mad
   c) It attracts them to the road, where a car can hit them

3) True or false: The main reason many species of animals are endangered is because they're really dumb.

4) If you want to protect flying bugs, one way to do it is:
 a) Give them a gun b) Cover the bottom of a porch light
     c) Build a little house and only let flying bugs in

5) True or false: The Yangtze River Dolphin is one of the most endangered animals on the planet because there are only about 100 of them left in the whole world.

6) True or false: One simple thing you can do to help protect birds is to buy organic bananas.

7) Why is it dangerous to animals if you throw plastic wrap that was covering food on the ground?

8) Whales are a treasure of the Earth. They're so big that a baby whale can drink enough milk each day to fill over...
    a) 300 bottles b) 2,000 bottles c) 50,000 bottles

9) True or false: The only place you can see a dodo bird is the tropical island of Bango-Bango.

QUICK QUIZ #4:
GARBAGE & STUFF

We need less garbage and more recycling. How many of these garbage/recycling questions can you answer? Answers start on page 205.

1) If you're an average American, how much garbage do you produce all by yourself, every single day?

    a) 2–4 pounds b) 10–12 pounds c) 4–6 pounds

2) What kind of recyclable material do Americans throw away the most?

3) Iron and steel are the most recycled materials in the world. But in the U.S., we throw out so much steel that we could use it to...

 a) Build a tower to Mars b) Play 1,000 games of magnetic tic-tac-toe c) Rebuild all of our new, American-made cars

4) Take a guess: Which material in the average recycling bin is worth the most money?

5) One of the highest points in Ohio is a man-made hill called "Mount Rumpke." What is this hill made of?

6) True or false: You can recycle paper milk cartons.

7) How many gallons of water would you save by recycling one ton of paper?

        a) 7,000 b) 70 c) 700

8) According to the U.S. government, how much of our garbage could we recycle?

      a) All of it b) 75% of it c) 50% of it

9) What can you help protect by recycling?

        a) Trees b) Mountains c) Me

THE ANSWERS

QUICK QUIZ #1 —Energy Use

1) *Unfortunately, false.* We *do* know a lot of ways to save energy…but few of us do many of them. Instead, we keep using more energy every year. What a waste!

2) *B—your refrigerator.* Unlike other appliances, it's running all the time, all year. 2nd place: Washing machine 3rd place: Clothes dryer.

3) *B—Turn down the heat, of course.* Heating and cooling use more energy than anything else in your home.

4) *Your home!* The U.S. government says that houses put out *twice as much* global warming pollution as cars! So you really can fight global warming by saving energy at home.

5) *True.* There so many places where heat can escape—cracks under the door, open fireplaces, and so on—that they add up to a big hole in the wall. Do an *energy audit* and see.

6) *True.* Electric cars save energy, cut pollution, and even cost less to run!

7) *False.* The sun is a reliable, renewable, cheap source of energy. Scientists are creating many ways to use its power!

8) *C—an appliance that's energy efficient.* The Energy Star program was designed by the U.S. government to help you tell which appliances make the best use of energy.

9) *B—You save a lot of energy.* Compact fluorescent bulbs are 10 times better at saving energy the regular bulbs.

QUICK QUIZ #2 —Using Water

1) *B—the bathroom.* About 75% of the water we use at home is used in the bathroom. About 20% is used for laundry and cleaning.

2) *False—it's more.* It's estimated that the average American family turns on the faucet between 70 and 100 times. Go to the tap and pretend to turn it on and off 100 times.

If your arm doesn't get too tired to keep going, you can start to imagine how much water your family uses. Now think of this happening in every house in the U.S., every single day!

3) A—*just a tablespoon!* Very, very little of Earth's water is drinkable. That why it's so important to take care of it.

4) B—*no more than a week.* You might live 3–4 weeks without food, but it's hard to last even a week without water.

5) *False.* Our faucets are an incredible luxury. Poor women in Africa and Asia walk an average of over 3 miles for water. In urban areas like Calcutta, India, people often have to wait in line at an outside tap to get water.

6) *True—about 1.1 billion people don't have clean water to drink.* And some 1.6 million people die each year from diseases in their water. Many are young children!

7) Somewhere between B(96) and C(175). It depends on where in the U.S. you live. But with conservation we could use a *lot* less!

QUICK QUIZ #3 —Protecting Animals

1) *False.* About 1,200 species are officially listed as threatened or endangered, but scientists think there are more than 6,500 species in the U.S. at risk of extinction.

2) C. Millions of animals are killed by cars every year.

3) *False.* The main reason animals are dying out is that we are destroying their habitats (places to live and have babies).

4) B. Bugs fly into porch light fixtures and get burned by light bulbs. One expert suggests attaching a piece of aluminum foil to the bottom of your porch light with a rubber band. But talk to your parents before trying this!

5) *False.* The Yangtze River Dolphin, which lived in China, is now considered "functionally extinct." None have been seen since 2007.

6) *Yes, it's true.* Birds that fly to South America in winter—called *migratory* birds—are poisoned by pesticides used on banana plants. So organic bananas help keep them healthy.

7) If plastic wrap has food on it, and you throw it on the ground, an animal might eat it. When plastic film gets in an animal's stomach, it can kill them.

8) *B—2,000 bottles*—enough to supply a human baby for a big part of a year! That's BIG!

9) *False.* You can't see a dodo bird anywhere, because dodos became extinct around 1681. See *en.wikipedia.org/wiki/Dodo*

QUICK QUIZ #4 —Garbage and Stuff

1) *C—4–6 pounds.* Keep track for a day or two, and see how much garbage YOU create.

2) *Paper.* It's estimated that 1/3 of our garbage is paper… and we could be recycling almost all of it!

3) *C*—we *could* rebuild all our new, U.S-made cars.

4) *Aluminum.* Experts say it's worth as much as $2,000 a ton. Yet we still only recycle about 45% of it.

5) *Garbage.* Really! It's one of the biggest landfills in the U.S., located north of Cincinnati. It's owned by Rumpke Consolidated Companies and is 1,045 feet above sea level.

6) *True AND false.* It's technically possible to recycle them, but the paper is coated with plastic, so hardly anyone does it. Where you live, this is almost certainly false.

7) *A—7,000.* We don't normally think of saving water by recycling, but factories use a lot of water to make things like paper. Saving paper means saving water, too!

8) *B—around 75% of it.* This includes food waste (which can be composted), paper, glass, and so on. But Americans only recycle about 32% of our garbage, so we still have a long way to go.

9) *All of them, including me.* By saving resources, we preserve our clean water and forests…and we keep the planet healthier, so people like me can live healthy lives. Hey, thanks for recycling!

Keep Going!

Check out our web site
50simplekids.com

The right spot
for great information,
cool web sites,
video links,
blogs, and plenty of
all-around eco-tips!